TEXTILE DESIGN

THEORY AND CONCEPTS

TEXTILE DESIGN

THEORY AND CONCEPTS

CHARU SWAMI

Independent Textile Design Consultant and Trainer
Agra, UP, India

NEW AGE REFERENCE

An Imprint of

NEW AGE INTERNATIONAL (P) LIMITED, PUBLISHERS

LONDON • NEW DELHI • NAIROBI

Bangalore • Chennai • Cochin • Guwahati • Hyderabad • Kolkata • Lucknow • Mumbai

Visit us at **www.newagepublishers.com**

Published by New Age International (P) Ltd., Publishers
First Edition: 2011
Reprint: 2017

GLOBAL OFFICES

- **New Delhi** **NEW AGE INTERNATIONAL (P) LIMITED, PUBLISHERS**
  7/30 A, Daryaganj, New Delhi-110002, (INDIA)
  Tel.: (011) 23253771, 23253472, **Telefax:** 23267437, 43551305
  E-mail: contactus@newagepublishers.com • Visit us at www.newagepublishers.com
- **London** **NEW AGE INTERNATIONAL (UK) LTD.**
  27 Old Gloucester Street, London, WC1N 3AX, UK
  E-mail: info@newacademicscience.co.uk • Visit us at www.newacademicscience.co.uk
- **Nairobi** **NEW AGE GOLDEN (EAST AFRICA) LTD.**
  Ground Floor, Westlands Arcade, Chiromo Road (Next to Naivas Supermarket)
  Westlands, Nairobi, KENYA, **Tel.:** 00-254-713848772, 00-254-725700286
  E-mail: kenya@newagepublishers.com

BRANCHES

- **Bangalore** 37/10, 8th Cross (Near Hanuman Temple), Azad Nagar, Chamarajpet, Bangalore- 560 018
  Tel.: (080) 26756823, **Telefax:** 26756820, **E-mail: bangalore@newagepublishers.com**
- **Chennai** 26, Damodaran Street, T. Nagar, Chennai-600 017, **Tel.:** (044) 24353401, **Telefax:** 24351463
  E-mail: chennai@newagepublishers.com
- **Cochin** CC-39/1016, Carrier Station Road, Ernakulam South, Cochin-682 016, **Tel.:** (0484) 2377303, **Telefax:** 4051304
  E-mail: cochin@newagepublishers.com
- **Guwahati** Hemsen Complex, Mohd. Shah Road, Paltan Bazar, Near Starline Hotel, Guwahati-781 008,
  Tel.: (0361) 2513881, **Telefax:** 2543669, **E-mail: guwahati@newagepublishers.com**
- **Hyderabad** 105, 1st Floor, Madhiray Kaveri Tower, 3-2-19, Azam Jahi Road, Near Kumar Theater, Nimboliadda Kachiguda, Hyderabad-500 027, **Tel.:** (040) 24652456, **Telefax:** 24652457
  E-mail: hyderabad@newagepublishers.com
- **Kolkata** RDB Chambers (Formerly Lotus Cinema) 106A, 1st Floor, S N Banerjee Road, Kolkata-700 014
  Tel.: (033) 22273773, **Telefax:** 22275247, **E-mail: kolkata@newagepublishers.com**
- **Lucknow** 16-A, Jopling Road, Lucknow-226 001, **Tel.:** (0522) 2209578, 4045297, **Telefax:** 2204098
  E-mail: lucknow@newagepublishers.com
- **Mumbai** 142C, Victor House, Ground Floor, N.M. Joshi Marg, Lower Parel, Mumbai-400 013
  Tel.: (022) 24927869, **Telefax:** 24915415, **E-mail: mumbai@newagepublishers.com**
- **New Delhi** 22, Golden House, Daryaganj, New Delhi-110 002, **Tel.:** (011) 23262368, 23262370, **Telefax:** 43551305
  E-mail: sales@newagepublishers.com

ISBN: 978-81-224-3053-0
C-16-10-9882

Printed in India at Glorious Printers, Delhi.
Typeset at In-house, New Delhi.

NEW AGE INTERNATIONAL (P) LIMITED, PUBLISHERS
7/30 A, Daryaganj, New Delhi-110002
Visit us at **www.newagepublishers.com**
(CIN: U74899DL1966PTC004618)

PREFACE

Clothing and Textiles is an enormously wide subject. At a rudimentary level, it deals with concepts such as textile fibres, yarn structure and fabric construction. At an advanced level it deals with concepts such as elements and principles of design, colour theories and various dyeing and printing techniques.

It is a difficult task for a beginner to gather relevant and reliable information from disparate sources. Therefore, a need for a well compiled literature at one source induced the author to write this book. The text of the book is written in a simple language and is supplemented with suitable illustrations for better understanding. This is a focused textbook, which would help the undergraduate students of Home Science Colleges and Polytechnics. The book is also positioned as a reference text for advanced readers in the field of clothing and textiles.

Extensive literature has been referred to prepare the book. The author acknowledges the support of various reference sources in exploring the main concepts, fundamental principles and the latest topics in the area.

The book encompasses five sections namely Overview of Textiles, From Fibre Structure to Fabric Construction, Techniques and Technology of Dyeing and Printing, Textile Design Process, and Contemporary Textiles. An attempt has been made to provide the basic information and clear, consistent presentation of the text on the above mentioned topics by incorporating appropriate images, pictures, diagrams and tables from various sources.

This book is an outcome of the effort to fill the need of a basic textbook in the field of textiles covering all the elementary topics in a single reference. The author hopes that this objective has been accomplished with the publication of this book.

The author acknowledges the support of all the individuals who have helped in this project to reach from the initial stage of conceptualization to the printing desk.

Charu Swami

ACKNOWLEDGEMENT

Successful completion of a task rests upon a complex interaction of various factors. Of these, inspiration and cooperation assume paramount importance. Therefore, I feel that it is my utmost duty to express my heart-fell thanks to all those who have directly or indirectly given me their valuable contribution with their blessings and cooperation to complete this task of mine.

At the very first instance, I take the redeemed opportunity to surrender myself at the feet of God Almighty who gave me infinite power by infesting sterling inspiration and efficiency within me to complete my task. At the very outset I bow to "The Supreme Father" for showering his blessings and grace on me.

I am deeply indebted to all my family members for their unflinching support and blessings. The affectionate help, sacrifice, encouragement, blessings and full cooperation of my family members played a significant role in accomplishing this task of mine.

I would be failing in my duty if I do not express my humble and deep gratitude to my husband Professor Sanjeev Swami for his inspiration which instilled a desire to complete this work successfully. I gratefully honor his motivational guidance at every stage of completion of this book. I offer loving thanks to my two children, Agam and Ami, for adjusting to my busy schedule and cooperating me throughout.

The author gratefully acknowledges the support provided by the immensely useful secondary data available on the URL's of various web sites available from time to time. I also wish to thank my co-author Ms. Reena Bhatia, my co-author in earlier version of the book entitled "Introduction to Clothing and Textiles".

Last but not the least, I take the opportunity to thank Mr. Saumya Gupta (Managing Director), Mr. L.N. Mishra, Mr. Rajpal and all others at New Age International Publishers who have helped in successfully printing this book on time.

Charu Swami

CONTENTS

OVERVIEW OF TEXTILES

Section I

Learning objectives:

By the end of this section, you will be able to understand:

- The meaning and definition of textiles
- History of natural and manmade fibres
- The general understanding of textile industry and fabric resources
- Various applications of textiles apart from the very common apparel and home furnishing

CHAPTER 1

HISTORICAL PERSPECTIVE OF TEXTILES

WHAT DO WE MEAN BY TEXTILES?

'Textiles are Pervasive.'

Textiles are indispensable part of human civilization. Textiles serve the individual, the home and the country. We are all aware that the prime needs of man are food, clothing, shelter and fuel.

The word Textile comes from the Latin word 'Textilis' and the French word "Texere" pertaining to weaving or to woven-fabric.

It covers all the woven materials whether made of wool, cotton, silk, jute, rayon or other manmade fibres. The variety of materials is simply tremendous.

Textiles are so much a part of our daily lives that it is not unusual that we take them for granted. The fabrics that clothe us can be considered a part of us, just as the air we breathe and the environment that surrounds us. In fact, textiles have created a stimulus for man's indigenousness and creativity since before the recorded history.

The recorded oldest indication of fibre usage comes with the discovery and spinning of flax and wool fabrics at excavation sites of the Swiss lake inhabitants in the 6th and 7th century BC (Refer Fig. 1.1).

Fig. 1.1 Early spinning wheel for flax spinning

The invention of sericulture began in China around 2640 B.C. and was introduced in India in times as ancient as 400 AD. While reports of spinning of cotton date back to 3000 BC. The cultivation date of Hemp, the oldest fibre plant that originated in south-east Asia, and spread to China, dates back to 4500 BC. (Refer Fig. 1.2).

Fig. 1.2 Women spinning with a wheel in early century

Similarly, the art of spinning linen and weaving was introduced by Egyptians in around 3400 BC (Refer Fig. 1.3) through their self developed tools and objects. (Refer Fig. 1.4)

Fig. 1.3 Egyptians at weaving process

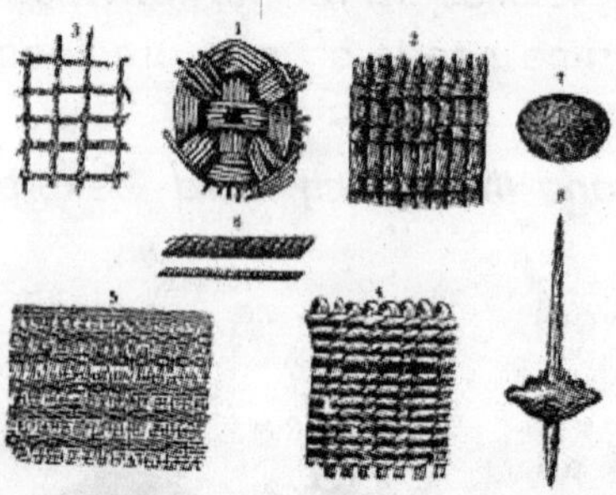

Fig. 1.4 Pre historic weaving tools and objects

By the time civilization reached ancient Egypt, textiles had reached such an advanced state of technology that the linen used to wrap mummies still remains preserved as textile materials. Through the following centuries textiles played a major role in civilization and world economics.

The 18th and 19th centuries witnessed an era of industrial revolution with invention of machines for processing various natural fibres. The result was a tremendous upsurge in fibre production. The introduction of regenerated cellulosic fibres (fibres formed of cellulose material that has been dissolved, purified, and extruded), such as rayon, followed by the invention of completely synthetic fibres, such as nylon, polyester, acrylic, challenged the monopoly of natural fibres for textile and industrial use.

A variety of synthetic fibres having specific desirable properties began to penetrate and dominate markets previously monopolized by natural fibres. The first commercial production started was of rayon fibres in America in 1910 and then further nylon fibre was introduced by the Du-Pont company in the year 1939. Since then multitude of fibres viz. Acetate, Acrylic, Polyester, Spandex, Polypropylene etc. have been incubated from various sources and chemical integration through intensive research and development. In this regard several Micro fibres are introduced. (A micro fibre is the thinnest, finest of all manmade fibre, even finer than the most delicate silk, and amongst the line is the most recent fibre introduced is Lyocell fibre [Tencel] in 1993.

Lyocell is a manmade environment friendly fibres produced from spieces of trees specifically grown for this purpose.

Recognition of the competitive threat from synthetic fibres resulted in intensive research directed towards the breeding of newer and better strains of natural-fibre sources with higher yields. Improved production and processing methods, and modification of fibre yarn or fabric properties and mechanization of textile machinery in this regard were also incorporated.

But, if we glance back through the pages of history, the mechanics of textiles have undergone rapid and creative evolutions and inventions. The world economy is imprinted with rich history of the textile industry and its evolution and progress since ages. Weaving is the one of the oldest crafts that has survived till date, dated back to the Neolithic ages, almost 12,000 years back. It is true that man's need for clothing since first signs of civilization and the spinning of wool fibre into yarn and then weaving of cloth is the basic step that has led to development of the new technology for the textile industry.

Now, if we refer to this one of most basic but important process of spinning, it can be divided into two primary stages. The fleece was opened to create a sliver of fibres which could be drawn out to produce an fine thread. It used to be then twisted into a yarn. It is known that people from early ages probably twisted fibres from a lock of wool to form an extending length of yarn which would then be wound up into a ball. The yarn was afterwards wrapped on to a stick and a flywheel added at the lower end to produce a spindle. This led to the development of spinning wheel in India first and then reached Europe during the late 14th century. This ancient spinning wheel was mechanized over the years and lead to spinning process being carried out on a large scales at mill level (Refer Fig. 1.5) **(Refer Plate 1.1)**

Fig. 1.5 Spinning machine

Thereafter, these yarns had to be assimilated together for construction of a fabric, the process termed as weaving. To serve this purpose a equipment that is loom was evolved.

The first loom is believed to have been simple with a straight tree branch running parallel to the ground. The lengthwise threads were hung from the branch, weighted at their lower ends and the widthwise threads interlaced to create a rough textured cloth. As time passed, the tree branch was replaced with a vertical framework, as were used by the Greeks (Refer Fig. 1.6). It was later switched to horizontal orientation. Later, the Egyptians are believed to have invented the shuttle for holding the horizontal set of yarns and to also have attached the vertical set of threads to two sticks in order to part the threads so that the shuttle could pass through. Keeping in line with the developments, various horizontal looms were crafted. These are prevalent till date, though with several modifications (Refer Fig. 1.7).

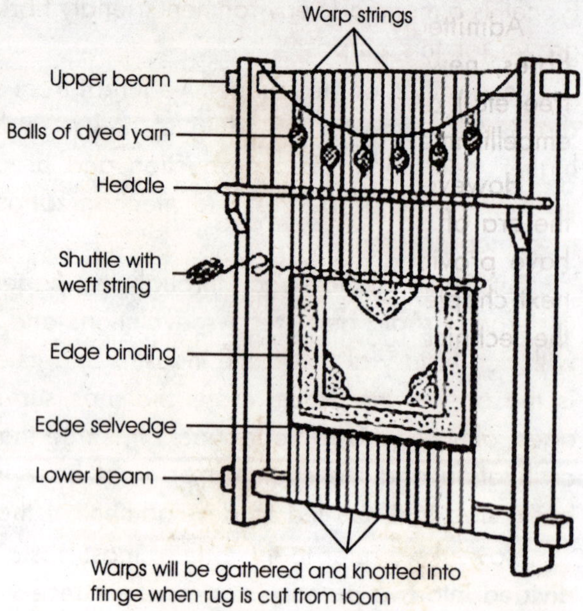

Fig. 1.6 Verticle loom

Fig. 1.7 An ancient handloom

Leonardo da Vinci is known to have designed a mechanical loom to be driven by water power during 1080 AD (Refer Fig. 1.8). The loom is of ancient origin, but the first modern invention to increase its efficiency was the flying shuttle patented by John Kay in 1733 **(Refer Plate 1.2)**.

Many important inventions took place during the 16th century , often having important spin-off effects on other parts of the overall process of textile manufacture. Invention of power loom resulted in greater production from a single loom, cloth of greater width. During the middle of 1780, Edward Cartwright invented the first steam powered loom to further enhance production.

The industrial revolution rolled social and economic changes and one of the social fear faced by people was that with the pace in technology and inventions of power looms, **(Refer Plate 1.3)** traditional hand weavers feared their livelihood. But this did not however hinder the developments in the textile industry.

Fig. 1.8 Leonardo da Vinci with his spinning wheel attached to a loom

Admittedly, during the past few decades, a new textile world has emerged. New fibres, new fabrics, new finishes (soil-resistant, light weight, permanent press, wrinkle free etc.) also new technologies for spinning, weaving and fabric ornamentation and embellishment have created new demands for understanding and evaluation of textiles.

However, despite the rapid developments in the field of textiles one cannot ignore the era of rich heritage and magic of traditional textiles since these traditional art forms have provided the foundation for the later development in the field. Therefore, in the next chapter we study these basic art and craft foundations and later move on to study the technical developments in this field.

CHAPTER 2

TRADITIONAL INDIAN TEXTILES

India has a rich cultural heritage of tradition, art, music, literature, sculpture and textiles. This exhibit unity in diversity through variegated charms of festivals, rituals, music, costumes and languages.

India is famous world wide for its magnificent workmanship, exhibited in the beautiful hand spun, and hand woven, dyed, printed and embroidered textiles. With their sheer beauty, colour and artistry, the artisans and craftsmen have woven their way to win the hearts of both royalty and the common people across the country. And with the wealth of knowledge and skills passed down from one generation of master craftsmen to the next, it will continue to do so for a long time to come. Stretched along the length and breadth of the country, every region has its own design, motif and characteristic fabric that weave its history, which is why there are hundreds of different textiles in India.

Let us now focus on few of the important traditional textiles of India.

BROCADES OF BANARAS

Extreme softness, vivid colours and translucent texture characterizes the silk weaving of Banaras. It is also known as Kashi or Varanasi and is one of the oldest inhabited places of the world. Alaipura is traditionally the district of Varanasi where the famous brocades are woven. Today they are woven in another parts of Varanasi also.

Brocades are textiles woven with the warp and weft threads of different colours and often different materials and usually are woven in silk and metal threads.

The sarees and fabric up to 6–10 meters are usually woven by muslim weavers known as 'karigars'.

The zari thread used is known as 'kalabattun' which is made of finely drawn gold or silver metals in yarns wound round a silk cotton thread core centre.

Traditionally, the design of the brocade was first worked out on paper. An expert called 'naksha bandha' rendered the design into cotton threads or a 'naksh'– a thread device that performs the same function as jacquard. Today the jacquard loom has replaced the use of the naksha.

The brocades of Banaras are divided into 3 types (Refer Fig. 2.1).

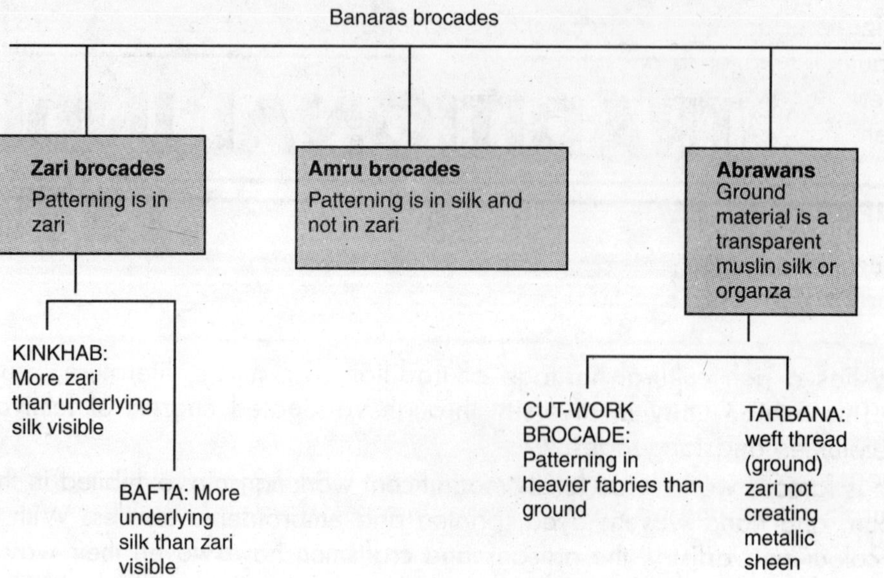

Fig. 2.1 Classification of brocades

(i) **Opaque zari brocades i.e.** Kinkhab, which are heavy brocades with more zari visible than the silk. Kinkhab was often used for furnishing and rarely for clothing. It was a proper trading article in the local market and was also exported to Europe.

(ii) **Amru brocades** are without any metal thread work. The supplementary weft woven for the design is silk and not zari. One distinct type of Amru brocade is 'Tanchoi'. This is a densely patterned heavy fabric. Many times the 'pallu' and 'borders' of a tanchoi saree are highlighted with zari.

(iii) **Abrawans** are transparent silk or organza woven; with or without zari. All over patterns are woven with a supplementary yarn. The floats on the backside of the fabric are cut-off later the weaving is complete. For this reason the abrawans are also called 'cut brocades'. Another kind is the tissue brocade with a combination of silk and zari yarns. This fabric gives a metallic sheen, known as "Tarbanas".

The motifs used for brocaded fabrics are paisleys, peacocks and floral patterns. The delicate designs of the past were replaced at the end or the 19th century by patterns taken from the Victorian era **(Refer Plate 1.4)**.

The Banarasi Sarees are deep coloured, laden with gold thread and form popular attire for the wealthy Indian brides **(Refer Plate 1.5)**.

Today brocades are still used by some for curtains and upholstery. Brocaded zari sarees and lehengas (long skirts) are still in demand for marriages, religious ceremonies and other auspicious and social occasions. Indian brocades are also in great demand abroad and foreign designers are designing garments of this material that blends itself so well to the creation of fantasies.

Looking back a hundred years, one is amazed to find that in spite of rapid industrialization, most of the age-old centers of handloom textiles still continue to produce these beautifully woven fabrics. The main centers besides Banaras are Ahmedabad and Surat where Benarasi sarees of the finest silk, gauze and gold with lively colour schemes are woven.

KANCHIPURAM SILKS

Kanchipuram in Tamilnadu is a famous temple around 50 km south of Chennai. Kanchipuram as the city is called, produces silks of superb texture, colour and luster. This textile is characterized by heavy use of zari.

The main items of production are silk sarees with brocade borders called the kanchipuram or kangivaram or the kornad sarees **(Refer Plate 1.6)**.

The glamour of the Kanchipuram silk saree lies in its colour contrasts. Pyramidical temple borders, checks, stripes and floral "buttas" are traditional designs, featured in a Kanchipuram saree **(Refer Plate 1.7)**. In a genuine Kanchipuram saree, the border, body and pallav are woven separately and then interlocked together. The joint is woven so strongly that even if the saree tears, the pallav (or border) will not detach.

The motifs used are floral (tiny patterns or creeping vines for border design), elephants, peacocks, double headed eagles and the kalash or the khumba motif. The colours are loud and bright combination like dark blue and magenta, parrot green and black, turquoise blue and orange, green and mustard are some of the favorite colour combinations of the local population.

PAITHANI SAREES

Among the most gorgeous of Indian sarees is the paithani, woven in the western state of Maharashtra. Exemplifying the merger of the aesthetic with the symbolic, they are today a prized possession and a family heirloom.

Paithan is village near Aurangabad in Maharashtra. The borders of the saree are prepared separately and are either total zari border with a different coloured silk pattern or zari design of a silk border.

The border and the 'reversible' pallav are the defining features of an original Paithani saree. The unique fact about the pallav is it is 'reversible' with the same design seen on both sides. **(Refer Plate 1.8)**.

The motifs used are interwining leaves and flowers, parrots, peacocks and even horses. Paisleys are rarely used **(Refer Plate 1.9)**.

The colours used are bright combinations like yellow-red and orange-green. The sarees, which are 9 meters long, are called the Navwari sarees and the ones, which are 5 meters are long, are called Pachwari. The Maharastrian bride always possesses a green paithini saree in her trousseau.

BALUCHAR BROCADE SAREES

Old undivided Bengal had ancient textile traditions, of skilled weaving. This includes the jamdanis of Dhaka and the Baluchar brocade sarees of Murshidabad. The ***Baluchar technique*** of weaving brocades with untwisted silk thread is based upon the miniature paintings of India. The specialty of the Baluchar sarees is the large pallav with a central pattern of flowing Kalgas, the mango design enclosed by repetitive frames of miniatures. These brocades never contain zari. The borders and pallav are decorated and woven with supplementary set of silk yarns **(Refer Plate 1.10)**.

The motifs used for the end piece are large paisleys, human figures, hunting scenes and scenes from the epics. The motifs are planed in separate boxes, which represent architecture.

The colour combinations used are:

(a) Base colour of the saree is dark and the colour of weft which forms designs is light e.g. black saree with beige or dull orange designs.

(b) The base is of light colour beige with dark designs of any one of the colours green, red, black.

These sarees always have only two colours thus creating a virtual effect of painting through weaving techniques.

JAMDANI SAREES

Dhaka, now is Bangladesh is famous for producing one of the finest muslins. These were referred to as 'air' or 'mist' by the English. Dhaka is famous for producing the finest and most expensive muslin sarees called Jamdani sarees.

The borders are either-1-1½ or 3-4 inches wide and are made by placing different coloured yarns with some decoration on them. The field is scattered with small buti designs. The end piece has 2 or 3 rows of motifs woven on it.

The Jamdani sarees are woven using a distinctive technique. Each motif is woven separately by hand using individual spools. This produces an opaque pattern against a transparent back ground **(Refer Plate 1.11)**.

Before partition these were woven in Tangail, now in east Bengal. The west Bengal Jamdanis are also called Tangail Jamdanis because they use the typical motifs of Tangail. The motifs are strictly floral and geometrical.

In terms of colour and design the Jamdanis could have either natural unbleached base with bleached white cotton thread motifs, or pastel coloured grounds with white motifs or a dark coloured grounds (black/blue/maroon) with white motifs **(Refer Plate 1.12)**.

The Jamdanis are believed to have given rise to the chikankari embroidery.

SANGANERI TEXTILES

Rajasthan is the heart of hand-block printing. Very close to Jaipur is Sanganer, the center for block and screen-printed cotton cloth. The Sanganeri block prints usually consist of floral motifs. Block printing has become popular because of the simple process which can create amazing prints in bold and vibrant colours **(Refer Plate 1.13)**.

The natural dyeing colours are used in Rajasthani Sanganeri prints. Yellow is derived from turmeric and buttermilk, green from banana leaves, black from iron rust, blue from indigo plants, red from sugarcane and sunflower and purple from the Kirmiz insect. The basic colours are scarlet, black and brown but now, with increasing technology and use of synthetic dyes, unusual combinations of scarlet and pink, purple and orange, turquoise and green are gaining market demand.

Sanganeri printing is done with the help of wooden blocks, known as chhapas or buntis found in different shapes and sizes. Blocks are made of seasoned teak wood with design on the underside of the block. These blocks are dipped into dye to print the pattern on the cloth. A flat earthen plate called the tariplate is used. Into this a bamboo rid called the "Katli" is laid. On the top of the Katli, is a felt fabric called "kambal or gaddi" is placed. The printing paste is poured on the felt piece. The katli helps the right amount of paste to seep through so that the extra paste does not smudge the edges of the block.

These wooden blocks have different floral motif carved on them. The design or the layout of the pattern is made using wooden blocks dipped in geru, a burnt sienna colour mixed with water.

The Sanganeri prints are always on a white background famous for its artistry and intricacy of design **(Refer Plate 1.14)**. Various floral designs, geometrical and god figures are included in its prints. Folk designs are found quite often and are famous, as they retain the basic Sanganeri printing style. Nowadays beside traditional prints modern designs are also found on block printed cloth.

The traditional skirts (ghagras) of Rajasthan carry these block prints in a very elegant manner. These skirts with added style have a place in the fashion world. Mostly, the furnishings, bed covers, curtains, cushions and bed sheets are demanded in Sanganeri prints. Beside, the dress material is also famous amongst not only the local people but world over.

BHAGRU PRINTING

Hand block printing, a handicraft that has secured a seat in the forefront of the fashion today. This craft has seen a major turn over the last two decades and has moved away from its traditional rural centers to the big fashion houses. The Bhagru and Sanganer are two important centers of block printing. The two printing styles are quite similar and prints cannot be easily distinguished. But each style has its own typical characteristics.

Sanganeri fabrics were more sophisticated; Bhagru products were aimed mostly at the local rural women. The designs ink both places reflect the persian influences.

Bhagru printing is a combination of resists style of printing and mordant resist style of printing. The resist style of printing is also called "Dabu" or mud resist printing which gives white designs on a coloured back ground.

It is done by chippa community of Bhagru village near Jaipur. Whereas the Mordant resist style of printing gives coloured designs Red/black with a dark blue/green background.

The basic concept of block printing remains the same for both the Sanganer and Bhagru prints. The wooden blocks made of teak wood are used for printing. The design to be printed is carved on lower side of these blocks, which are dipped in the required colour of natural dye. The beautiful designs, easy designing process and use of natural colours have made Bhagru prints very important in Rajasthan's block printing. Also, Bhagru prints are very famous among the traditional look of the wear and ethnic taste of the furnishings **(Refer Plate 1.15)**.

Bhagru is also famous for textile prints but printers in Bhagru use vegetable colours and use different motifs. Where, the Sanganer prints are always on a white background, Bhagru prints are essentially in deep and dark shades. The Bhagru prints excel in circular designs and zig-zag motifs done in dark vegetable colours. Bed spreads, table linen and other furnishings are mainly demanded in Bhagru prints.

KALAMKARI

Kalamkari is an exquisite ancient craft of painted and printed fabrics. It derives its name from Kalam meaning Pen, and Kari meaning work, literally pen-work. It is hand painting as well as block printing with vegetable dyes. Kalamkari art has evolved through trial and error over the last 3000 years. Techniques of craftsmanship in Kalamkari were handed down within the families from generation to generation.

Kalamkari that is painting on the fabric is done in several parts of India and Iran. In Andhra Pradesh, both the Masulipatnam and Srikalahasti villages are recognized as major centers for Kalamkari painting.

The coromandel coast of India stretching from Masulipatnam in the north and Nagapatnam in the south was historically the source of some most beautifully coloured and delicately worked cotton fabrics exported by India in the 16th century. These cotton fabrics were called 'pintado' meaning painted by the Portuguese and 'chintz' by the English.

The King of Golconda (near Hyderabad) had links with the Persian king and these fabrics were exported to Iran. Thus lot of Persian influence is seen in the art of kalamkari.

Today kalamkari is done at 2 main centers (i) Sri Kalahasti and (ii) Masulipatnam both in Andhra Pradesh.

Both these places have distinctive styles of their own.

(i) *Sri Kalahasti:* Sri Kalahasti has been ruled by the Hindu rulers. Kalamkari here was done on wall hangings for temples and shrines. Scenes from the Mahabharata and Ramayana were depicted. Gods, mainly Lord Krishna is done in blue, women in yellow and demons in deep re/black. Telugu script is written in between the lines to describe the painting.

(ii) *Mauslipatnam:* The muslim rulers ruled this place. Hence they were forbidden to use any human or animal designs. They used exotic flowers from the Kashmiri shawls and carpets. Mythical flowers and geometrical motifs were also used. Tree of life, is a very popular motif, which originates from one point or a pot, is proportionate and symmetrical and has exotic birds and flowers. Paisley is another very commonly used motif.

The Kalamkari art of painting undergoes a laborious, slow process of resist-dyeing and hand printing. Many stages are undertaken before the final results are achieved. Unlike other styles of painting, Kalamkari painting demands a lot of treatment before and after the painting is completed on the cotton fabric. Depending on the treatment of cloth, or quality of the mordant, the colours change accordingly. Every step from soaking of the cloth, to sketching the outlines to washing and drying the cloth, is done carefully and correctly.

In line with the other traditional textiles, the harmless, natural dyes are used for Kalamkari paintings. The natural dyes, are extracted from bark, flower and root. The colour red is obtained by using the Indian madder root, yellow from the pomegranate seed or even mango bark, and black from myrobalan fruit. No chemical dyes are used is producing kalamkari colours.

The process used for both types of Kalamkari paintings is more or less the same. The only major difference is that Srikalahasti paintings depend entirely on the brush-like pen whereas the Masulipatnam style uses block-printing procedures. The process done in Srikalahasti is more tedious **(Refer Plate 1.16)**.

A common procedure involved in both is as follows:

1. The cloth is first whitened by immersing in a solution of goat or cow dung and letting it dry in the sun for a few days.
2. The cloth is then treated in myrobalan solution. Ripe fruits are used in Masulipatnam, raw ones in Srikalahasti. Milk is then added to the solution to prevent the colour from spreading in the next step.
3. The Kalam is made out of a bamboo reed, which is hollow. This is pointed at one end and is 6-8" long. At the sharpened end a felt pad is placed which holds the dyestuff. Pressure applied by the finger, releases the dyestuff, which travels down to the point of the Kalam. More the pressure applied, more dyestuff is released.

Outlines are first drawn free hand with charcoal. The black outline is painted by putting iron acetate into the hollow area of the kalam. If certain lines in the design are red, alum and; water are filled in the kalam. Filling of the designs is done by applying the mordant with a brush. The brush is prepared by flattening and softening a bamboo stick at one end. Then iron acetate solution is filled in, either for solid spaces or as outlines, with a brush-pen in srikalahasti, and wooden blocks in Masulipatnam.

4. All the areas meant to be red are painted or printed over with the alum solution as a mordant. Mordant is a substance that fixes the natural dye on the material.
5. After applying alum, the cloth is kept for at least 24 hours. Then the excess mordant is removed by washing the cloth under flowing water.
6. The dyeing is done for the red colour by boiling with the red colouring materials.
7. All the portions that are not to be blue are covered with wax.
8. The waxed cloth is then immersed in indigo solution. In srikalahasti, the blue is painted with the kalam. Then the wax is removed by boiling the cloth in water.
9. The yellow is painted on to blue to produce green.
10. The cloth is finally washed again and dried before the final colours emerge.

MITHILA PAINTINGS

Perhaps the best known genre of Indian folk paintings is the Mithila (also called Madhubani) paintings from the Mithila region of Bihar state. For centuries the women of Mithila have decorated the walls of their houses with intricate, linear designs on the occasion of marriages and other ceremonies. The kohbar ghar paintings (Painting on the walls) are based on mythological, folk themes and tantric symbolism, though the central theme is invariably love and fertility.

The contemporary art of Mithila painting was born in the early 1960's, following the terrible Bihar famine. The women of Mithila were encouraged to apply their painting skills to paper as a means of supplementing their meager incomes. Once applied to a portable and thus more visible medium, the skills of the Mithila women were quickly recognized. The work was enthusiastically bought by tourists and folk art collectors alike. As with the wall paintings, these individual works are still painted with natural plant and mineral-derived colours, using bamboo twigs in lieu of brush or pen.

These wall paintings were done on thick hand made paper and were recognized as 'madhubani painting' by the All India Handicraft Board. The printing press form where the Mithila village got their paper is situated in the town Madhubani. Thus the name Madhubani painting.

The Mithila paintings are divided into

Wall paintings–Khobar-ghar-for weddings and Gosain ghar for Durga Ashtami.

Floor paintings–called Aripan

Motifs–for khobar-ghar are lotus; bamboo, snake, birds, fishes, brides and wedding ceremony–for gosain ghar are goddess Durga, goddess Kali, and scenes from the epics **(Refer Plate 1.17)**. Motifs for the aripan are large geometrical and floral motifs. Other motifs are scenes from daily life, and pan ka patta etc. The centre of the area to be painted is identified and a dot is placed there. Growing outward from this dot the entire motif spreads to the periphery of the space.

Traditionally, the women of Mithila used pigments derived from natural substances, viz. vermilion powder (sindur), with mustard seeds gave a bright red colour, cow-dung and lamp black gave greyish black, turmeric gave yellow ocher-indigo, green, red clay were mixed with gum to provide blue and Indian red.

Today chemical pigments are sourced from Calcutta. These powder colours are mixed with goat milk to produce the liquid paint instead of goat milk, gum or fevicol are also used. Thin bamboo twig is used to make the outline. A thick bamboo with a rag tied at one end is used for filling up larger areas, usually with bright colours thus and producing an enchanting art form.

IKAT TEXTILES

The word Ikat is derived from a Malaysian word 'mengi ikat' which means, "to tie". The areas of production in India are Patan, Surat and Rajkot in Gujarat; Pochampalli, Guntur and Chirala in Andhra Pradesh; Sambalpur, Cuttack and Balasore in Orissa.

Ikat fabric is an artistically ornamented fabric. It is a wonderful combination of the craft of tying & dyeing alongwith weaving which is synonymous with the word "ikat". The basic technique followed for the production of ikats is the tie and dye of the yarns. In Andhra Pradesh and Orissa either the warp or weft yarns are tied and dyed to make the Ikat design. This is called warp ikat and weft ikat respectively. In Gujarat the designs is formed by tyeing and dyeing both wrap and weft yarns. This is called double ikat e.g. Patola. The procedure of producing these two ikats also differs, which is described below:

1. In Gujarat, silk is used but in Andhra Pradesh and Orissa both silk and cotton yarns are used as raw material. All the raw material is in the form of undyed yarns.
2. The warp or weft threads or both are divided into bundles, and tied with water proof material like cotton threads, rubber strips, leaves etc. to correspond with a pre arranged design.
3. The bundles are then dyed; tying threads resists the colours of the first dying and the yarns are redyed. More the number of colours more are the number of successive tying and dyeing. The lightest colour is dyed first and then darker and darkest for successive dyeing. The ties are opened after drying the yarns.
4. The warps are then arranged on the loom and the pattern is aligned according to the design. The wefts are wound on the shuttles. Once the warp threads are put on the frames, the design becomes visible. The warps are then sized to maintain their tension.
5. Weaving is done on a very simple horizontal loom. The weave is always a plain weave. Any other kind of weave will disturb the tie and dye pattern of the threads. The weaving process is so accurate that the warp design and weft design overlaps to form a motif.
6. The final arrangement of warp and weft threads is done with an iron needle which is the size of a pencil. The weaving progresses at the rate of 6-8" per day. The whole procedure is labour intensive land requires immense patience.

Motifs used in Gujarat ikat are flowers, jewellery, elephant, tiger, parrot, dancing woman, betel leaf. Geometrical designs like squares with flowers or jewels are made for the muslim community.

Double ikat is used to give definite outlines of the design. The famous Patola silk sarees are made using this technique.

In Orissa, cotton and tassar silk are used. Either warp ikat or weft ikat is done to make lungis, dupattas, sarees and blouse pieces, bed covers, cushion covers, and yardage is also made. The only place were double ikat is done in Orissa is Sambalpur, which produces the famous Sambalpuri saree. The motifs used are shells, fish, tortoise, serpents, chess board (called pasapalli, chaupad), geese (Hansa), khumba (Kalash), flowers, rice seeds and sum. The Orissa ikats have a white outline around the design **(Refer Plate 1.18)**.

In Andhra Pradesh, Chirala, a coastal village is famous for the production of ikat cloth known a Telia rumals also called Asia rumal. These rumals are used by the muslim men to tie on their heads and are exported to Middle East, Africa, Pakistan, Bangladesh and Burma. The size of the rumal is 55 × 77 cm. There are eight rumals in on yardage and is called "than". These rumals are dyed with traditional alizarin dyes. This leaves an oily smell (sesame oil is used ink dyeing) on the fabric and has hence got the name Telia from "Tel" (Oil).Telia rumals are also called chitkirumal (locally) have a distinct colour scheme based on red, blue/black and off white. Outer borders are red; with blue or black centre having off white designs. Outer borders are blue/black with a red field having off-white designs. Double ikat technique when used for the central field makes the rumal expensive. For lower classes single ikat warp/weft pattern is adopted.

The motifs used are geometrical and floral only. Sometimes, Islamic, motif of moon and star is also used. The patterns and colours of the telia rumals have been adopted on sarees, dupattas and lungis called Telia sarees, Telia sarees, Telia dupattas, and Telia lungi respectively **(Refer Plate 1.19)**.

Pochampalli is another place in Andhra Pradesh where cotton ikat, sarees and lungis are woven, the motifs are again geometrical and floral. Either warp or weft ikat is used for producing; usually Pochampalli sarees **(Refer Plate 1.20)**.

BHANDHANI OF GUJARAT AND RAJASTHAN

Bandhana or Bandha are Sanskrit words which mean "to tie"; the reason why Bandha work is called Bandhini. Internationally, the tie and dye work is known by a Malaysian name of "plangi", 'Bandanna', an English term is derived from Bandhana which is a spotted handkerchief.

Jamnagar, Rajkot, Porbander, Kutch and Anjar in Gujarat and Bikaner, Sikar, Jodhpur, Jaipur, Udaipur and Nathadwara in Rajasthan are the main centres of tie and dye work in India.

Tie and dye is a form of resist dying on fabric. Here the designs are resisted by tying threads on the pre designed areas, after which the fabric is dyed; thus called tie and dye **(Refer Plate 1.21)**.

These textiles are produced by elaborate but straight forward process; which is as follows:

1. The fabric is washed in caustic soda and water.

2. The fabric used to tie and dye is very fine e.g. mulmul, silk, chiffon. These fabrics are folded into 2 or 4 parts. The design areas are marked only on the 1/2 or 1/4th part of the fabric with the help of wooden locks.
3. The fabrics are tied with a cotton yarn. The material is pushed up from beneath with along pointed nail of the little finger of the left hand, or a spiked metal ring is used. The protruding fabric is wound 6–8 times. The thread is not cut and is led on to the next tie. This goes on till all the design areas to be left white are tied.
4. The fabric is always dyed with the lightest colour first, usually yellow. It is squeezed and dried. The pattern, which is to appear yellow is tied and then dyeing, is done in a darker colour, such as red/green. After drying, the fabric is again tied on the designs, which are to show red/green. It is then dyed in even darker colours like maroon, black, dark brown and dark blue.

The parts of the cloth that are not to be dyed in the darkest colour are wrapped up tightly in plastic to resist the dyeing.

In Rajasthan, the tie-dye stuff sold in the markets is not untied, to show that it is genuine bandhini and not a print. The pimpled effect is appreciated and left un-ironed. In Gujarat the fabric ties opened and the fabric is starched and ironed **(Refer Plate 1.22)**.

Techniques of tieing

- Tieing the fabric in different ways can show various interesting end results.
- A little fabric lifted with a fingernail and tied result in a dot **(Refer Plate 1.23)**.
- The fabric is knotted at the intervals **(Refer Plate 1.24)**.
- The fabric is crumpled with hands and rolled haphazardly into a ball and tied with threads all around. This is called marbelling **(Refer Plate 1.25)**.
- Stitch resist or tritik: Any design is made and running stitch is done on the design and the thread is pulled tightly. Two rows of running stitch give a better outline. Most common motif done ink this way is the cowrie or 'kodi'.
- Lahariya: The fabric, usually very fine mulmul is folded and tied out intervals with threads and dyed. This leaves a striped pattern on the fabric. These striped look like waves called 'lehar' in Sanskrit **(Refer Plate 1.26)**.

Motifs used for Bhandhani are—bindi (dot), Laddu (circle) dabbi (rhombus), and Ras mandala (women dancing in a circle around a centre medallion). The bindi is used to make elephants, peacocks, flowers and geometrical shapes; using bright, colourful and varied colours in cotton and silk for different end products like apparels, sarees, home-furnishings etc.

Thus, more or less every state in India is known for a particular indigenous textile of that state. These traditionally woven fabrics in India crafted by skilled weavers, on handlooms, are associated with several craft traditions , such as Mirror work of Kutch and Kathiawar, Punjab is known for its traditional floral embroidery called Phulkari work. Further North Kashmir is known for fine handmade embroidery in wool and silk, on woven woolen shawls and garments known as Kashida embroidery. Uttar Pradesh is famous for white embroidery on pastel cotton garments called Chikankari from Lucknow to name a few, which enhances the surface appearance of the woven fabrics, thus increasing its appeal and economics too.

Overflowing with colour, texture and designs, India's textile heritage and cultural diversity is visible in its traditional textiles. The colour, the feel, and the smell of textiles captivates one in this era multifaceted arts and crafts which have now further flourished through the following centuries and played a major role in civilization and world economics thus adding to the versatility of textiles.

CHAPTER 3

VERSATILE APPLICATIONS OF TEXTILES

Textiles are the most ancient and the most modern industries. These are among the magical products of the high-tech world of the late twentieth century.

There is an infinite variety of fabrics of different textures, colours, pattern and designs at our disposal, providing a shopper's paradise for the customer; at the same time making the task of consumer difficult in judging the quality, serviceability, durability and suitability of the materials for different purposes or for its end uses. Specifically, the cotton fabric ranges from thick coarse sail-cloths to the finest dress materials. The mention of wool brings to mind finest suitings and dress materials on one hand and a host of domestic materials such as blankets on the other. Earlier jute was used in making of sacks for packaging, now-a-days even apparels are possible. While, nylon products could be as light as book cloth, umbrella fabrics to something as heavy as tyre cord.

The textiles provide us comfort appearance and have varied end uses in every field of life. The versatility of textiles is truly remarkable **(Refer Plate 1.27)**.

While apparel and home furnishings are the best known end uses, textiles are also used in an extremely wide range of other products. Examples of these special uses include artificial blood vessels, bulletproof vests, civil engineering earthwork construction, artificial turf, industrial filters, space vehicles, and as structural and reinforcing components in automobiles and aircraft. In larger sphere it helps serve our country through specialized fabrics in army, navy, aeronautics and in manifold industries. The most recent field that has evolved as a major textile application is the field of technical textiles. (www.bch.in).

Technical textiles include industrial textiles, performance textiles, engineering textiles and high technology textiles. The world consumption of technical textiles is projected to increase manifold each year.

Technical textiles are high performance textiles that require special functionality. The market of technical textiles is significant and expanding as the products are being put to an ever-increasing number of end uses in various industries such as agriculture, clothing, construction, health care, transportation, packaging, sports, environmental protection, protective wear, and many more.

The global market for technical textiles was estimated to have a volume of 16.7mn. tonnes with a value of US$ 92.88 billions in the year 2000 and is expected to grow to a volume of 23.77mn. tonnes with a value of US$ 127 billion by the year 2010. In developed nations technical textiles holds a share of more than 40% of the total textile manufacturing activity. While the US and EU continue to be the main manufacturers and consumers of functional textiles, China has emerged as a large manufacturer of the same.

India and Russia are the other important markets for technical textiles, where consumption is increasing at a fast pace.

THE INDIAN SCENARIO

In the present scenario, technical textiles has been identified as a great potential area for upgrading the Indian textile industry. Since the conventional textiles industry has reached a level of saturation in terms of development, innovation and value-addition, technical textiles offer a great opportunity to succeed. Secondly as the country is transforming into a developed nation, huge emphasis is being laid down in adopting latest technologies and procedures in various fields. Therefore the market for technical textiles is very positive and poised for a stupendous growth. Attractive statistics for market potential seem inviting for global intervention.

Considering that India has a large pool of skilled and scientific/technical manpower, it can play a major role in shaping the future of this industry. Development of new fibers and technologies has led to the creation of new applications of technical textiles, which is bound to enlarge the market size and offer opportunities for high growth.

Here these technical textiles are classified on the basis of various **industries** they cater to, thus accounting to numerous end uses of textiles **(Refer Plate 1.28)**.

CONSTRUCTION TEXTILES

Civil engineering and building industry are an integral part of the development of human society as they involve the planning, design, building, operation and maintenance of infrastructure. The venturing of technical textiles or high-performance textiles in this sector has given a great impetus to the quality of construction.

These textiles are used in the construction of buildings, dams, bridges, tunnels and roads. They offer mechanical properties such as lightness, strength and resilience as well as resistance to many factors such as creep, degradation by chemicals and pollutants in the air or rain and other construction material as well as the effects of sunlight and acid. These textiles play an important role in the modernization of infrastructure.

Some of the major products covered under this sector are used in:

- Hoardings and Signages
- Scaffolding nets
- Awnings and canopies
- Tarpaulins
- Architectural membranes
- Roofing materials.

ECO TEXTILES

Environmental threats loom large on almost every nation in the world today. With this threat gaining its stature day-by-day, Eco Textiles gain utmost importance as one of the most useful resources that help promote new innovations, in an eco-friendly manner.

These eco-friendly textiles provide a range of environmentally responsible alternatives to other resource hungry materials. They tap into both post-consumer and post-industrial waste streams & scrap and reuse them for manufacturing an extremely durable and eco-friendly textile. They not only lead to reduction of waste but also more importantly, save the rapidly depleting natural resources.

Eco-friendly textiles utilize ecologically grown fibers and are processed in a manner which saves energy and reduces waste output.

The products that are produced through the eco-friendly textiles are:

- Soil seals
- Textile drainage systems
- Erosion prevention systems
- Textiles for protection against hazardous substances
- Mobile containers
- Textile noise barrier systems
- Filter systems (air/water), Landfill textiles etc.

AGRO TEXTILES

Agriculture has been amongst the most primal occupations of the humankind. In this era of modernization and high technological advancements, it has spread its horizons and started using manmade, non-conventional textiles, called "technical textiles".

This textile sector comprises of all textiles that are used in growing, harvesting, protection and storage of either crops or animals. It includes diverse items such as fishing nets and fish-lines, ropes, shade fabrics, mats, woven and non-woven covers for crops, bird protection nests, etc. These textiles are driving the sector profitably by improving the productivity and reducing the need for chemicals.

Some of the purposes for which these textiles are being increasingly used are as follows:

- Preventing erosion and paving way for afforestation
- In greenhouse cover and fishing nets
- For layer separation in fields
- In nets for plants, rootless plants and protecting grassy areas
- As sun screens (since they have adjustable screening) and wind shields
- As packing material and in bags for storing grass (that has been mowed)
- Controlling stretch in knitted nets
- Shade for basins
- Anti-birds nets
- Fabrics for sifting and separation, for the phases of enlargement of the larvae materials for ground and plant water management at the time of scarcity and abundance of water.

CLOTHING TEXTILES

Touching our lives in almost all the spheres, technical textiles have also made their foray in the clothing and shoe industry. Aimed at fashion designers, developers as well as shoe and clothing manufacturers, this category of smart textiles includes technical components of clothing (such as breathable membranes), shoe reinforcement & construction as well as rainwear. They are recognized for some of their important properties like high resistance to temperature, pressure and other extreme conditions, high absorbency, durability and water proof nature.

From industries like sports, defense and aviation to chemical and fire fighting, they are making their presence almost across all segments as they are extensively used for making special purpose clothes and footwear.

The application in this sector is:

- In shoe components like shoe laces
- For insulation and structures like interlinings-(woven as well as non-woven, waddings etc.)
- Sewing products like sewing threads, labels, fasteners (zips, Velcro).

GEOTEXTILES

Geotextiles are smart textiles that consist of a stable network that retains its relative structure during handling, placement and long-term service.

Geotextiles are special fabrics made for use in 'geological' situations. They are rot-proof and permeable to water. They can be heavy duty or light duty, black, white or coloured. They are either in woven and non-woven forms and apply to a broad range of civil engineering construction, paving, drainage and other applications.

Geotextiles are extensively used with soil, rock, earth or any other geotechnical engineering-related material, as an integral part of humanmade project, structure or system.

- A glimpse at some of the many application areas:
- Roadways, parking lots, loading areas and construction sites
- Prevent drainage systems from clogging with fine particles
- Filtration, protection and separation function
- Fluid transmission
- For waterway erosion control
- Reduce soil piping
- Prevention of weed growth (in horticulture applications)
- Moisture conservation (in horticulture applications).

HOME TEXTILES

Seen as a mightily expanding and changing sector in the global textile industry, the presence of technical textiles is not merely confined to industrial applications but also in our day to day activities as well.

One of the largest technical textile markets, consumer textile sector comprises of household textiles, furnishings and upholstered furniture industry (including fiberfill and wadding applications in bedding, cushions, sleeping bags and furniture backings).

Some of the highly useful applications of Home textiles include:

- Woven and knit wipes (cleaning wipes for domestic applications)
- Non-woven wipes (floor mops)
- Tickings (for filled products like pillows, duvets, cushions)
- Mattress components (flanging and quilt backing, spring wrap)
- Spring insulators flat fabrics (used to cover springs in beds or upholstery)
- Platform cloth (fabrics used as a base for cushions on upholstered furniture)
- Dust cloths fabrics attached to base of furniture
- Skirt linings and other fabrics for use in upholstered furniture, bedding etc.
- Carpet backings (used as primary as well as secondary backing for tufted carpets)
- Sewing threads used in all furnishing, household textile applications.

INDUSTRIAL TEXTILES

The smart characteristics of technical textiles make them an ideal resource for use in various industrial applications like filtration, conveying, cleaning etc. This arena of technical textiles contains solutions and products for mechanical engineering and for varieties of industries, e.g. conductive textiles and 3-D textile products.

Widely used in woven, non-woven and knitted form, these industrial textiles are increasingly being used in almost all the major industries, like paper, carbon, metal, ceramic, glass fiber, plastic etc., across the globe. Some of the popular applications include:

- Dry and Wet filtration applications
- Polishing cloths
- Needle punched felt
- Drive belts conveyor belts (for paper making and food processing)
- Loop and eye fastenings
- Coated/laminated fabrics
- Fusing threads and rods
- Heat resistant yarns/fibers
- Coated and extruded yarns
- High tenacity yarns.

MEDICAL TEXTILES

Due to major technological developments, technical textiles are extensively used in the healthcare industry today. In the field of medical application, technical textiles are not just used in contact with the skin, but also fulfill important functions within the body (implants). Technical textiles offer medical and hygiene industry with unparalleled protection, comfort and cost saving.

These highly specialized and bio-compatible technical textiles, vary depending on the task for which they are to be used. Special antimicrobial finishes are an important characteristic of these textiles, along with absorbancy and impermeable properties.

Depending on the nature of application, most of the medical products are disposable in nature and are made of non-woven fabrics. In global markets disposables are fast replacing non-disposable health care textiles. Some areas of usage of medical textiles are:

- Healthcare/hygiene products-Include bedding, clothing, surgical clothes, products for feminine hygiene like sanitary napkins, baby and adult diapers etc.

Non-implantable materials-for wound care that includes absorbent pad (wound contact layer, base material viscose, plastic film) and bandages (simple inelastic/elastic, orthopedic, plasters, gauzes, lint, padding).

Implantable materials-like sutures, soft tissue implants, artificial tendon (meshes), artificial ligament, artificial cartilage, orthopedic implants artificial joint, cardiovascular implants vascular grafts, heart valves.

Healthcare/hygiene products-include bedding, clothing, surgical gown clothes, filters, bandages, support and protective material, surgical sutures etc.

PACKAGING TEXTILES

Packaging textiles include all textile packing material for industrial, agricultural and other goods. The demand for packing material is directly proportional to economic growth, industrial production and trade as goods are produced and then distributed both locally and internationally. The growing (environmental) need for reusable packages and containers is opening new opportunities for textile products in this market. Sacks and bags made of traditional jute, cotton or natural fiber are gradually casting way for modern synthetic fibers.

It is well known that these fabrics are ideal for many kinds of packaging. At one end, technical textiles for packaging includes heavyweight, dense woven fabrics (used for bags, sacks, flexible intermediate bulk carriers and wrappings for textile bales and carpets) and on the other end, it includes lightweight non-wovens used as durable papers, tea bags and other food and industrial product wrappings.

The use of textile materials in consumer packaging is exhibited in the following products:

- FIBC big bags (Flexible Intermediate Bulk Containers),for powdered and granular materials
- Laundry bags and other bulk packaging products
- Sacks for storage etc.
- Twine and string for tying packages, etc.
- Non-paper tea bags and coffee filters
- Food soaker pads
- Net packaging for storing, packing, transporting, retailing foodstuffs, toys,
- Woven fiber strapping, lightweight mailbags.
- Soft luggage.

PROTECTIVE TEXTILES

Defense/civil defense are industries which rely heavily on technology. Apart from hi-tech weaponry and ammunitions, the induction of technical textiles in this sector has revolutionized the concept of security. It is the new range of chemicals and fabrics being used by the armed forces that has redefined safety parameters for the military.

The protective clothing covers garments and accessories intended to protect people from dangerous or hazardous materials and processes during the course of their work or leisure activities. These textiles enhance performance by ensuring wind or water proofing, flame retardancy, breathability, lightness etc. in clothing used by firemen, Para-military forces and security forces. The major applications of technical textiles in this field are:

- Tents, sleeping systems, weapons rolls, to combat foul weather
- Fire service equipment, bullet-proof jackets, army tents, parachutes, extinguishing blankets, tubes
- Fabrics with waterproof and breathable membrane
- Mountain safety ropes, climbing harness
- Protective clothing fabrics for protection from fire, bullets etc.
- Special jackets, attire to combat severe temperatures
- Fabrics for disposable garments worn to provide protection against harmful chemicals and gases, pesticides etc.

SPORT TEXTILES

Technical textiles have enabled production of materials that are tougher than wood, which breathe like skin, are waterproof like rubber and at the same time are eco-friendly and highly economical. The growth in the sports and leisure industry have resulted in the use of technical textiles in different sports.

Today's sports demand high performance equipment and apparel. These high-functional and smart textiles are increasingly adding value to the sports and leisure industry by combining utilitarian functions with wearing comfort that leads to achieving high level of performance.

- A few areas where these textiles are being increasingly used are:
- Material technology and design of equipment
- Biomechanics and the engineering aspects of sports machinery
- Surface treatment of equipment
- Sportswear
- Sports footwear
- Artificial turfs, sleeping bags, ballooning and parachute fabrics

Some of the sports where these textiles are being used are Golf, Tennis, Cycling, Mountaineering, Skiing, Cricket etc.

TRANSPORT TEXTILES

Among other sectors, the automotive industry is one of the largest single markets for technical textiles and one of the most diverse as well. This market comprises of automobiles, trains, marine vehicles and planes.

The latest developments in aircraft, ship building as well as motor vehicle and train manufacture, all can be largely attributed to technical textiles in the field of transportation., which is a non-apparel textile.

It today covers not only isolation and safety aspect but also focuses on comfort and style. The customers look for aesthetically pleasing interiors, great comfort and fuel economy.

Textile components in automobiles consist of either visible components like upholstery, carpets, seat belts, headliners etc., or concealed components like tyre cords, hoses, belts, airbags etc.

Some of the applications in this industry are:

- Air bag fabrics
- Tyre cord fabrics
- Automotive upholstery and other textile fabrics used inside the vehicle
- Tyres, Engine
- Composites for body and suspension parts
- Comfort and decoration

Since, the textile industry has become so versatile it is difficult to understand the textile industry and its functions. This industry is a vast complex made up of many segments. Its distribution patterns are complex. The resources vary greatly in size and type. Therefore it is first important to get acquainted to the main sectors and functions of the industry.

MAJOR SEGMENTS OF THE TEXTILE INDUSTRY

The textile industry is a group of related industries using many different raw materials and making a great number of products. The following are considered the major production segments and are the basics of the textile industry.

Fibers

Fibers are the smallest part of the fabric. They are fine hair-like substances, categorized as either natural or manmade. Cotton, which grows on plant, and wool, which is shorn from a sheep, are two examples of natural fibers. The manmade fibers are created from chemicals, and include acrylic, nylon and polyester. They are produced by chemical companies, such as E.I. du Nemours and company and Monsanto company, Du Pont, Reliance Industries, to name a few.

Yarns

Most textile materials contain yarns. They are continuous thread-like strands composed of fibers which have been twisted together. (Felt would be an example of a material made from fibers but containing no yarns.) There are various types of yarn, from dull to slubby and lustrous. Each one could be made from different fibers. Yarns are used to produce fabrics.

Fabric Production

Most fabrics are either woven or knitted. The companies that make the cloth are called mills. The range of fabric types and weight is tremendous, fulfilling a variety of consumer demands.

Dyeing and Printing

Colour is usually applied to fabric by either a dyeing or printing process. The purpose is to make the fabric more appealing. These operations are performed in dye plants or print plants, and the companies are called dye houses or print houses.

Finishing

Most fabrics need additional treatments called finishes before they can be used. For example, special chemicals are used to make a water-repellent fabric suitable for a raincoat. A special brushing machine is required to make the fuzzy surface found on flannel fabrics. The processes are done in finishing plants whose facilities are most often part of dye plants or print plants.

MERCHANDISING AND MARKETING OF TEXTILES

Each segment of the textile industry must plan well ahead of the next retail selling season. Unless schedules are maintained and deadlines met by the fiber producers, fabric mills and other textile companies, goods will not be able deliver at the right time of the season. The time problem is especially acute in the textile industry since there are so many operations that must be performed before finished fabric is made. A delay in any of the operations will extend the fiber-to-fiber time period.

The textile and apparel industries are working towards reducing the time periods in order to respond more quickly to changes in the market place. One method is the use of electronic and internet/web link textile mills, apparel manufactures and retail stores for faster interchange of sales, delivery and inventory information. Other methods include shorter production runs, the use of the latest technology for faster textile and apparel production, as well as the use of computers by designers as a time saving device.

Therefore, further in this book we will have the in-depth coverage of all these major segments of the textile industry.

FROM FIBRES TO FABRICS

Section II

Learning objectives:

By the end of this section, you should be able to understand:

- Fibres, as basic unit of fabric
- Its basic properties and classifications
- Different procedures for spinning fibres to form a yarn; different yarn structures and their features
- Various methods of fabric construction with special reference to weaving

CHAPTER 4

TEXTILE FIBRES

Fibre is a "Building Block" of all textiles, just like bricks are for a building. Fibres appear in natural sources (animal hair, plant stems, leaves) or can be chemically made (nylon, polyester, acrylic); to name a few. In a very simple term—

"Fibres are the basic raw material of which fabrics are made".

Fibres are the basic and most fundamental components/units used in the making of yarns and fabrics. According to textile technologists, a fibre is defined as the raw material used in the manufacture of textile. It is a slender filament or a fine strand of sufficient length, strength and pliability to be spun into yarn and woven into fabric.

Some fibres are short, others very long, some are kinky, scaly and rough, others are straight and smooth. They may have high or low strength or are transparent, opaque, coloured or colourless, even or uneven in diameter. i.e., there are individual differences. Thus, the textile technologists have classified a fibre into three types on the basis of length.

1. A ***fibril*** is a very small cell or a component of a fibre cell wall and is customarily measured in microns or millimicrons (1 micron = 0.001 mm)
2. A ***fibre*** (Staple) is short in length and measurable in inches. The length varies between ½ – 24 inch. All natural fibres except silk are staple fibres, however even manmade fibres are cut into short lengths and then they are also known as staple fibres.
3. A ***filament*** is natural (silk) or manmade, which is spun or an extruded fibre or continuous length, measurable in yards or metres. It ranges between 400 yards –1300 yards.

Apart from the parameter of Length, if a fibre is to qualify for textile industry, these basic requirements must be met

- Availability in sufficient quantity.
- Economical in cost or have excellent relative value for use in certain textiles.
- Have satisfactory fineness to be readily spinnable.

For manmade fibres two additional requirements are as below

- Costly chemicals and solvents must be recoverable for re-use.
- By product must be marketable and waste must be disposable at low costs (This is applicable for natural fibres too).

Therefore, for a fibre to function well, it must have the following properties:

(a) Primary fibre properties
(b) Secondary fibre properties

Primary fibre properties:

1. *Length:* Fibres must be much longer than they are wider to permit any kind of use. Various fibres have different lengths; e.g. the length of cotton varies between 0.3" – 2" and wool between 1.5" – 12". Upper limit is immaterial because it can be easily twisted and made longer. Lower limit, for spinnability is at least 1 cm. i.e 0.4 inch. preferred on commercial scale otherwise 5mm. or 0.2 inch. is the limit, in regular case. All manmade fibres are made into very long filaments during its manufacturing process, so they do not require falling in this limit.
2. *Strength:* Fibres must be strong enough to withstand not only the mechanical operation of spinning, weaving or knitting but, other physical and chemical process. i.e. dyeing, bleaching, finishing and still give satisfactory service in wear. It should have enough strength when dry as well as wet. Strength with inextensibility is brittle, thus making it unsuitable for wear i.e. flexibility, softness, suppleness, elasticity are the properties should be present in the fabric, with regards to the ability to withstand repeated stress in actual service and recovery from creasing and distortion. Strength is the ability to withstand or resist breakage as a result of stress. It is expressed as *tensile strength* in terms of force/unit of cross-sectional area i.e. kg./sq. mm. or as *tenacity* in terms of strength/unit number (indicating the fineness of the fibre). Its unit is gm./denier.
3. *Pliability or Flexibility:* This property in a fibre is necessary for its easy moulding and twisting for spinning and further comfort during wear.

4. *Cohesiveness:* In order to have good spinning quality this property of cohesivessness i.e. clinging or sticking together in a mass is important. Lack of cohesion may result in uneven blending. A fibre with high degree of smoothness and uniform surface would not possess this. Also, more rigid a fibre, lesser the cohesion. Cohesiveness prevents fibre slippage. Cotton and Wool fibres display good cohesiveness property.
5. *Uniformity:* For making of yarns it is important that fibres should be similar in length and width. Fibres of uniform dimensions spin better and make uniform yarn which will produce uniform fabrics and give good service.

Secondary fibre properties:

1. *Physical Shape:* Average fibre length, surface texture, irregularities and cross-section constitute the physical shape of the fibre. The final appearance and use of fibre depends on the relative physical shape of the fibre.
2. *Density:* Density refers to the weight of the fibre as compared to water. Heavy fibre will sink in water and light ones will float contributing to the comfort and laundering care properties of the fibre.
3. *Colour:* Natural fibres like wool and cotton range from grey – brown – cream in colour. This may interfere in the dyeing process. Therefore the natural colours are bleached to white before they are dyed to any other colour. Whereas in case of man made fibres, the desired coloured filaments are obtained by adding the dye pigments in pigment solution.
4. *Elasticity:* Elasticity is the ability of a stretched or deformed fibre to return immediately to its original position upon removal of stress.

   Elongation: Elongation is ability of the fibre to be stretched, lengthen or extended.

   Elastic Recovery: Elastic recovery is the ability of the fibre to recover from strain or stress immediately or over a period of time.

These properties make the fabrics pliable, wrinkle resistant, and help to maintain their shapes and sizes.

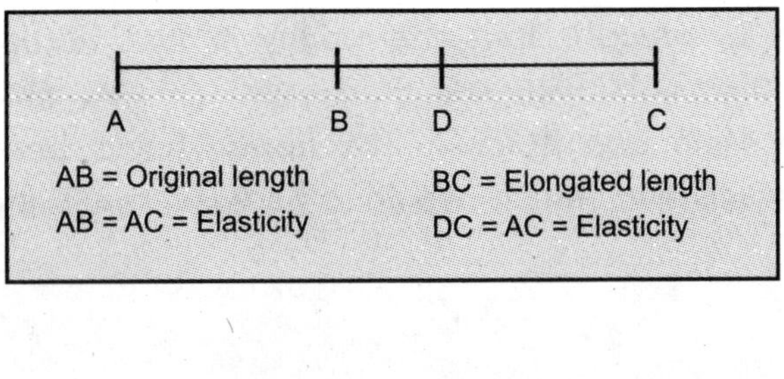

5. *Resiliency:* It is recovery from creasing. It is the ability of a compressed fibre to spring back to its original position on release of compression load. Resiliency is required for carpets, pillows, mattresses. A good elastic recovery means a good resilience. Wool is a highly resistant fibre.
6. *Crimp:* It refers to the waves, bends, twists, coils or curls of a fibre, that occur along its length. It has a direct effect on the yarn and fabric manufacture. Crimp serves specific end-uses such as comfort, absorbency (holding air and offering thermal insulation), bulk and warmth of the fabric. Crimp should be permanent and return after extension, distortion, wetting etc.

   Example: Wool has a natural crimp. Textured yarns (with crimp) are created to achieve more loftiness for carpets, sweaters, suiting, socks etc. Fibre crimp increases cohesiveness, resiliency, abrasion resistance, stretch, bulk and warmth, but, reduces luster. It is expressed as percentage of the stretched fibre length.
7. *Abrasion Resistance:* It is the ability of fibres to withstand rubbing, subject to everyday use. Usually it occurs at knees and eblow portions in case of apparels.
8. *Pilling:* Is forming of tiny balls of fibres ends on the surface of the fabric after being subjected to abrasion over a period of time.
9. *Lustre:* It is the light reflected from the surface of the fabric. It differs from shine because it is more subdued. Here light rays striking the surface are broken up whereas in shine the light rays are reflected only in one direction. It is an ornamental/aesthetic property rather than a necessity.
10. *Absorbency:* It is the ability of the fibre to take up moisture from a standard atmosphere (70^0 F and 65% RH) and is expressed as moisture regain in percentage. This property differs from fibre to fibre and contributes towards warmth and comfort.
11. *Dyeability:* It is the ability of the fibre to take up dye or colour.
12. *Dimensional Stability:* It is the retention of the fibre to its size, shapes and form.
13. *Feltability:* It is the ability of the fibres to mat together by the application of heat, steam and pressure. Example, woolen blankets.
14. *Thermoplasticity:* It is the ability of the fibres to soften and melt on heating. The fibres that exhibit this characteristic are called thermoplastic fibres. Example: Nylon, Polyester.
15. *Resistance to Chemicals:* It is the ability of the fibres to resist damage in presence of chemicals such as, Acids and Alkalis, etc.
16. *Resistance to Moth and Mildew:* The fibres should be resistant to the attack by moth and mildew, which would otherwise result in fibre degradation.

The above mentioned secondary properties are desirable in the fibres, but not essential, as in the case of primary properties.

Next, we would study in details about the basic unit of textiles i.e. "the fibres".

FIBRE CLASSIFICATION

The system used for the classification fibres is based upon the following categories:

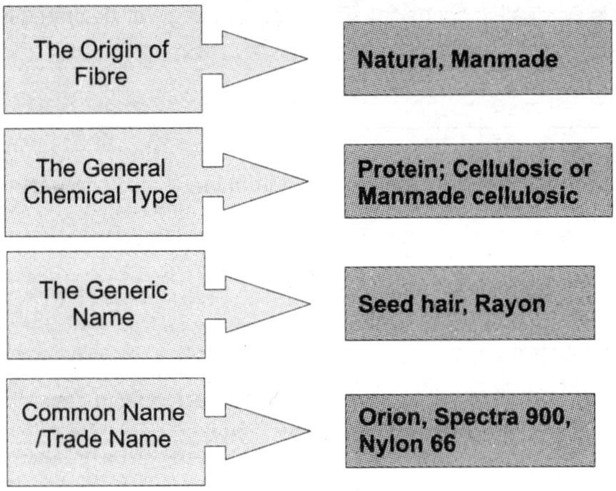

We will now briefly focus on some major textile fibres in each category **(Refer Plate 2.1)**.

NATURAL CELLULOSIC FIBRES

Natural Cellulosic fibres are of vegetable/plant origin. This includes cotton, wool, jute, flax, ramie, hemp, banana fibres to name a few.

COTTON: *"the seed hair fibre"*

The word cotton is derived from the Arabian word "Quoton" or "Qutun" which means a plant found in conquered lands. The origin of cotton is unknown. Archeological data suggest that cotton grew in Egypt in 12,000 BC, and in India is about 3000 BC. Cotton is grown all over the world. America (Texas, Arizona) South America (Brazil) Egypt and India.

The cotton plant belongs to the family *"Mal Vacea"*. It grows in warm climates both dry and humid. Cotton fibres appear in the seed pods, which burst open, thus exposing the fibres **(Refer Plate 2.2)**.

Processing of cotton fibre:

1.
Cotton is picked with hands as well as machines from the fields. Hand picked cotton results in better quality of cotton fabric.

↓

2.
After the cotton has been picked, it's taken to the gin for cleaning and purification. The fibre is now called cotton lint. The operation of gin is illustrated in Fig. 4.1

↓

3.
The gin separates the seed from the lint. Apart from that it also separates twigs, leaves and dirt The seed is valuable and is used to make cattle feed and cotton seed oil.

↓

4.
The cotton is packed into balls at the gin and the balls are graded according to the colour (ranges from brown-gray-off white), fibre length and the time when picked.

↓

5.
The balls are then shipped for making yarns and fabric.

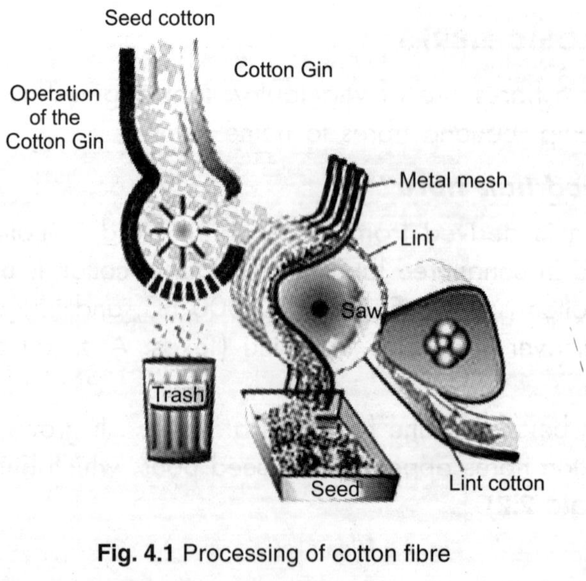

Fig. 4.1 Processing of cotton fibre

Fibre properties:

The microscopic ***longitudinal view*** of cotton under microscope appears like a twisted ribbon with twists or convolutions and thick irregular edges.

The ***cross-sectional view*** resembles the seed structure consisting of primary and secondary wall with a cuticle and a lumen present in the central portion (Refer Fig. 4.2).

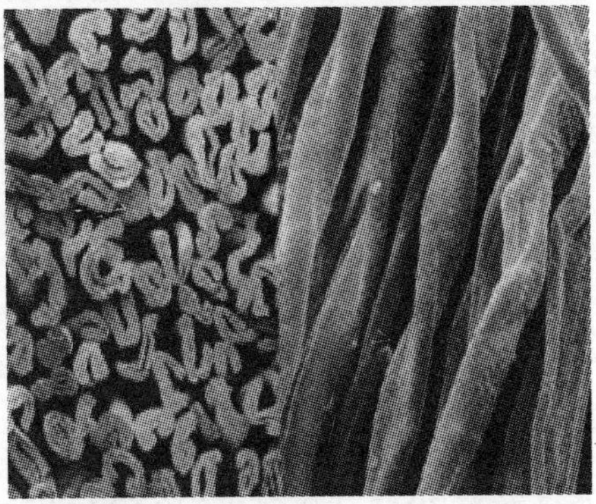

Fig. 4.2 Microscopic view of cotton fibre

"Kapok" & "Coir" are the minor fibres in the category of natural cellulosic fibres. Kapok is obtained from the seed of Java Kapok or the silk cotton tree and used as a fibre fills in pillows and life saving jackets. Coir is obtained from the fibrous mass between the outer shell and the husk of the coconut. Coir which is very stiff is used for the production of rugs, mats, floor tiles, bags, hats, and belts etc.

FLAX/JUTE: *"the golden bast fibre"*

Flax is a bast fibre. It is obtained from the stalk or stem of the plant linum usitatissimum. It is one of the old textile fibres. It is grown in western Europe-Belgium, France, Italy, U.K. and Germany **(Refer Plate 2.3)**.

Jute was used as fibre in the biblical times to make sack cloth. It is obtained from the inner bark of the corchorus plant. It is 61% cellulose and is one of the cheapest textile fibres. It is grown throughout Asia, chiefly in Bangladesh and East India **(Refer Plate 2.4)**.

Fibre properties:

Longitudinal view/cross-section

The microscopic structures of all the bast fibres are similar and has heavy striations along its longitudinal view while the cross-section is polygonal in nature (Refer Fig. 4.3).

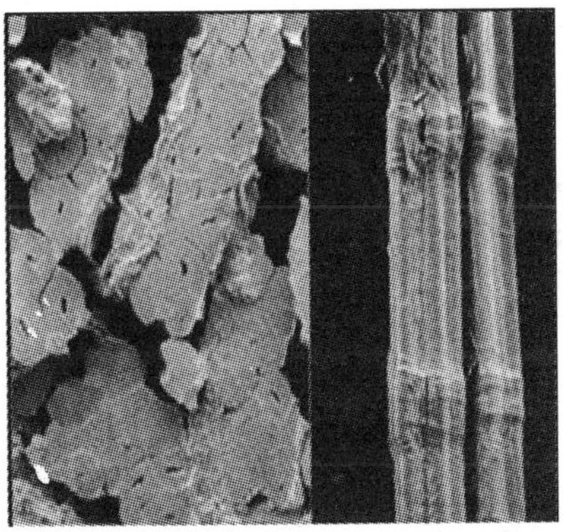

Fig. 4.3 Microscopic view of flax fibre.

Processing of Jute/Flax Fibres:

1\.
The stem for the fibre is pulled out by hand or machines while the roots are still intact or else the fibres get permanently discoloured. Stems are passed through special machines to remove seed pods which is a process of rippling.

↓

2\.
Retting is a process to remove outer woody portion of the stalk to obtain the fibre. Retting can be done by three methods viz. Dew retting (in fields), Water/Pool retting (in stagnant ponds/ pools), Enzyme or chemical retting (by NaOH).

↓

3\.
After the outer woody portion of the stems has rotted during retting, scotching is a process in which stems are dried and passed through the metal rollers which crushes the woody portion and the fibres are exposed.

↓

4\.
The fibres are combed to remove any remaining woody portion and arrange them in a parallel fashion through hackling or combing. This also helps in separating long & short fibres.

↓

5\.
The fibres are then drawn into yarns and spinning procedures is carried out.

↓

6\.
Lastly cottonizing is done to reduce the bast fibre to the length similar to that of cotton fibre. These cottonized fibres can be processed on equipment designed for cotton. All the bast fibres – jute, flax, ramie, hemp can be cottonized.

This process is illustrated in Fig. 4.4

FLAX TO FABRIC

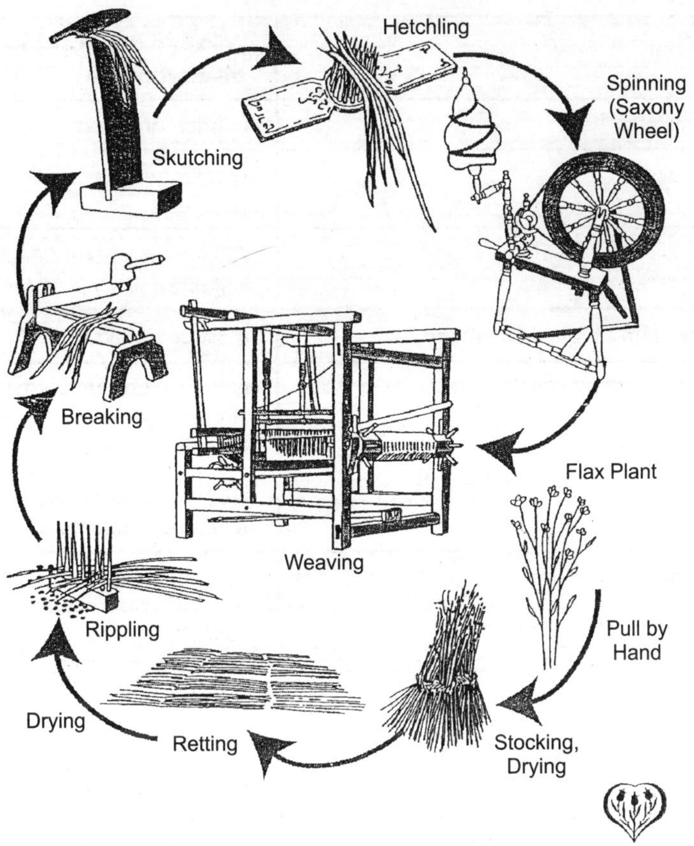

Fig. 4.4 Processing steps involved in converting flax to fibre

Jute is creamy white to brown in colour. It has poor elasticity and length therefore is easily subjected to snagging and splitting. Jute is used to produce sugar and coffee bagging, carpet backing, rope and cords but is facing stiff competition from olefin fibres for these end uses. Burlap or Hessian (terms used for jute in the furniture industry) is used for window treatments area rugs and wall covering. Jute is also used for casual apparel and clothing in recent times.

Hemp, Ramie, Kenaf and other leaf fibres like Pina, Abaca, Sislal have various end uses like ropes, papers, mats, bags etc. including apparels as a result of various researches being carried out on them. Thus, these minor fibres are becoming the promising fibres of the future.

All the natural cellulosic fibres have some basic similarities and reactions because of having a common chemical structure and properties. This in turn offers certain advantages and disadvantages to the consumers.

Basic properties of natural cellulosic fibres:

	Properties	Relative advantages and disadvantages
1	Good conductor of heat	Fabrics are wearable in summer.
2	Low in resiliency	Fabrics wrinkle badly unless finished for recovery.
3	Absorbent	Absorbs moisture though less than cotton; suitable for summer wear.
4	Can withstand fairly high temperature	Must be ironed with a moderately hot iron.
5	Not greatly harmed by alkali	Fabrics can be bleached, washed with strong soaps; not greatly damaged by perspiration.
6	Harmed by acids	Fruit stains must be removed immediately to prevent setting.
7	Attacked by mildew	Avoid putting away soiled damp garments.
8	Not attacked by moth	Simplifies problems of storage.

NATURAL PROTEIN FIBRES

Natural protein fibres are of animal origin. This includes the hair (Wool, speciality hair, fur) and secretions of animals (silk, spider silk). Protein fibres are composed of amino acids containing carbon, hydrogen, oxygen and nitrogen. The protein present in wool is known as keratin, whereas that of silk is fibroin.

WOOL: *"the wonder fibre"*

Sheep skin, i.e. Wool, and other hair fibres were discovered before the fibres could be spun into yarns. The main areas of wool production are United States, Australia, some parts of India and the other regions which rear sheep and hair animals.

Processing of Wool:

1. To provide the finest quality of wool, the sheep are treated against diseases, given good nutritious diet to produce healthy animal so that the quality of wool is good.

↓

2. The sheared wool from a living animal is called fleece or clipwool and that from the slaughtered animal hide is called pulled wool.

↓

3. The newly removed wool is raw wool or grease wool and contains between 30 and 70% by weight of impurities such as sand, dirt, grease and dried sweat. The wool is scoured to remove these impurities with warm soapy water and weak alkali.

↓

4. Grading is done for evaluating the whole fleece for fineness and length.

↓

5. Carding and combing is done to prepare the wool fibres for spinning procedures. This process is illustrated in Fig. 4.5.

↓

6. Sorting is done to separate different qualities of wool. The best quality wool comes from the sides, shoulder and back and the poorest quality wool comes from the lower legs **(Refer Plate 2.5)**. Fineness, color, crimp, strength, length and elasticity are characteristics that may vary with the breed of sheep.

Types and Kinds of Wool:

The term wool legally includes fibres from sheep, angora and cashmere goats, camel, alpaca, llama and vicuna.

(i) Lamb's wool: Comes from animals less than seven months of age.

(ii) Virgin Wool: Wool that has never been processed.

(iii) Recycled wool: Scraps of woven or felted fabrics which are shredded, sorted, cleaned, re-spun and woven.

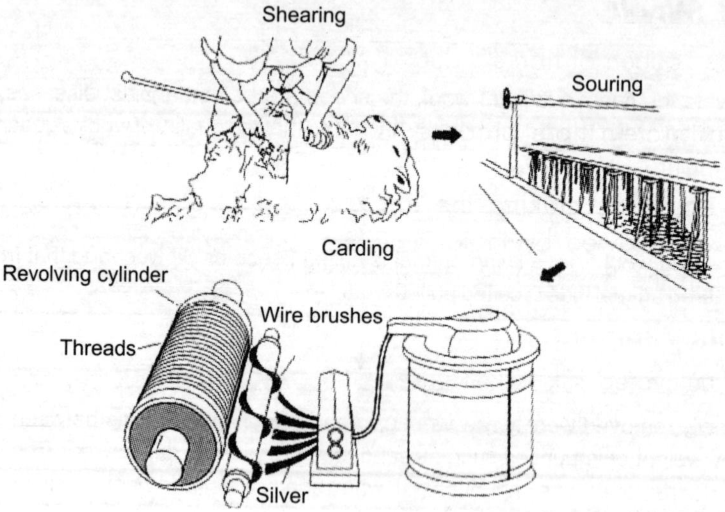

Fig. 4.5 Carding process of wool

Fibre Properties:

The microscopic ***longitudinal view,*** shows the presence of 'y' shaped scales on the fibres. The presence of these scales in the wool fibre structure attributes to certain physical features like shrinkage, matting and felting of wool (Fig. 4.6).

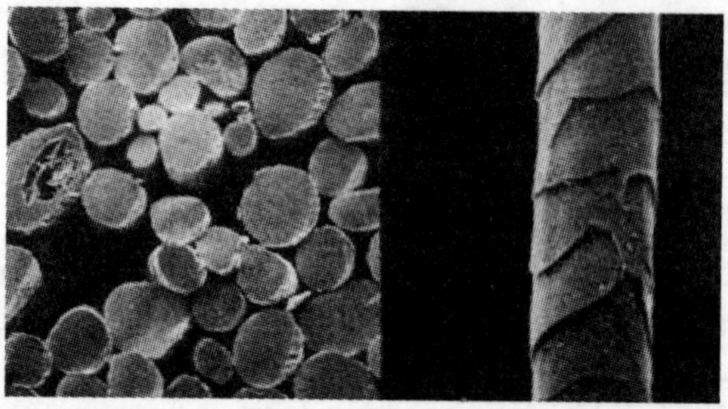

Fig. 4.6 Microscopic view of wool fibre showing a scaly structure

Wool is widely used for a variety of apparels all over the world. It also used for making carpets, rugs and blankets. The wool fibres trap air and form an insulating layer for the body thus making wool a warm fibre. It has also natural crease resistant and absorbent properties making it comfortable to wear.

Care of wool is difficult because it has tendency to matt up. The scales present on the wool fibre entangle with each other forming into google like structure. This causes the matting and thus shrinkage of wool. This property of matting is responsible for production of felts, a technique through which blankets and other non-woven goods are produced. Wool fibre is highly resilient in nature and has got a natural crimp along its fibre length thus contributing to the bulky and elastic characteristic of the woolen garments.

SILK: "queen of fibres"

Silk is known as "queen of fibres", due to its association with royalty, rich texture and appearance.

Silk is a natural protein fibre produced by the larvae of the silk moth. It is said to have been accidentally discovered in China and produced there for many years till China was discovered thus making the famous "silk route". China till date produces maximum silk (54%), followed by India (14%) and Japan (11%). In India, the southern states are involved in the Research & Development of silk cultivation and production.

Production of Silk Filament:

The production of cultivated silk is known as ***Sericulture.***

1.
Silk is produced by the larvae of several moths but Bombyx Mori is the only one raised under controlled conditions to produce silk (i.e. cultivated silk).

↓

2.
The female silk moth (Bombyx Mori) lays between 400-700 eggs. When the eggs hatch, the larvae are fed on mulberry leaves, These look like caterpillars, about ¼" long and are called silk worms. The larvae feed on the leaves for about 25-35 days and then become 3" long **(Refer Plate 2.6)**.

↓

3.
The silk worm attaches itself to a straw frame and begins to secrete the silk fluid which hardens on contact with air. The larva spins moving its head in a figure-eight motions and constructs a cocoon around itself. These cocoons can be stored till they are unreeled. The fibre that the larvae reels around itself to make the cocoon is coated with a gummy substance called sericin.

↓

4.
Silk filaments are unwound from the cocoons in a manufacturing plant called filature. Several cocoons are placed in hot water to soften gum. The insect inside dies. The ends of the filaments are then reeled on to a wheel. A uniformly reeled silk is more expensive than the one with joints.

↓

5.
Next is the process of throwing in which the filament from 3-8 reels can be combined together by inserting a twist. Thus is called a throw yarn.

↓

6.
Lastly is the process of Degumming through which sericin the gum present in the silk is removed. Sericin remains in the fibre during reeling and throwing, thus has to be removed by boiling the silk in soap and water. This is important for finishing and dyeing procedures.
This processing of silk fibre is briefly illustrated in this Fig. 4.7.

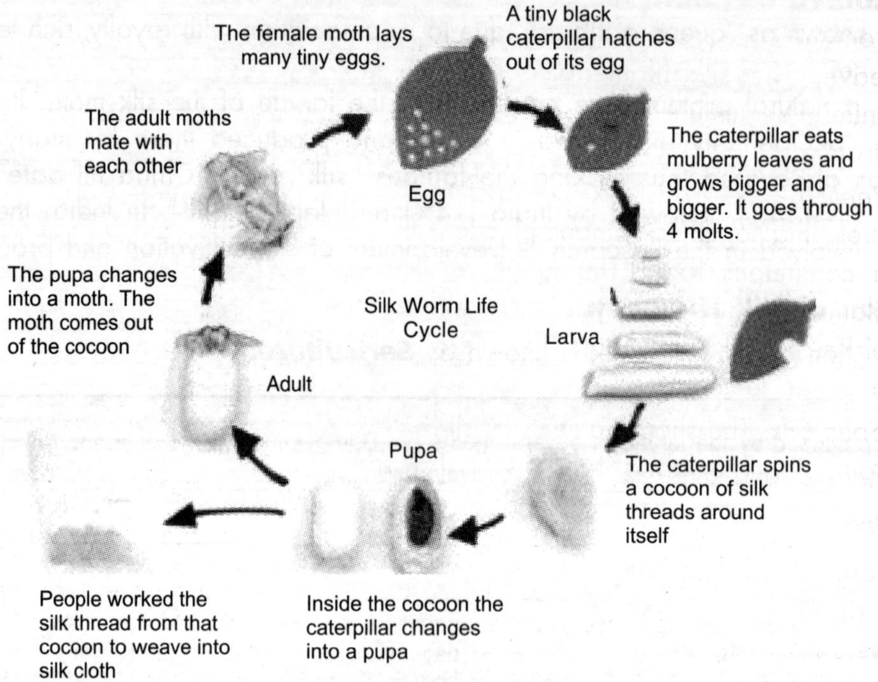

Fig. 4.7 Reeling process of silk

Types of Silk:

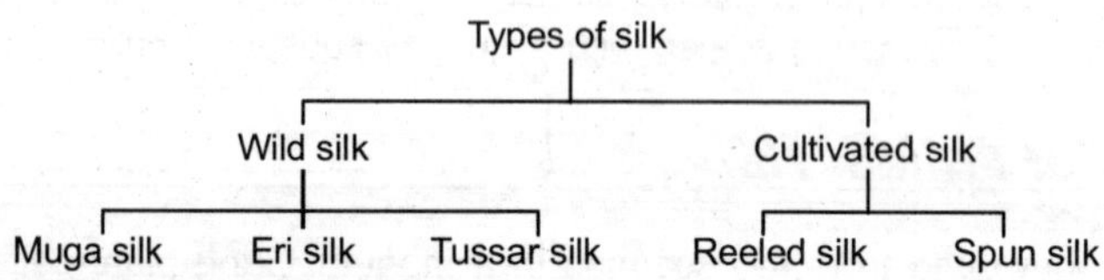

(1) **Wild Silk:** The production is not controlled. The silk worms are fed on oak and cherry leaves. The filaments obtained are not uniform in texture and colour.

(a) *Muga Silk*: The cocoons of Muga silk harvest on oak leaves. The silk obtained contains tannic acid which is present in oak leaves. Hence the Muga silk is hard, heavy and of low quality.

(b) *Eri Silk:* The cocoons of Eri silk are soft, white/yellow in colour. The silk obtained, thus is very fine and is soft in texture. This silk is usually obtained from Bengal and Assam.

(c) *Tussar Silk:* The cocoons are harvested on colocacia leaves, a tree commonly found in Central India. The silk obtained is brown in colour and has rough texture.

(2) **Cultivated Silk:** The silk is obtained from the cocoons that harvest on mulberry leave. The silk filaments obtained are uniform in texture and colour and appearance.

(a) *Reeled Silk:* This silk is obtained by stretching together number of cocoons in a continuous form. The length of these filaments is 300-1800 yards. The filaments of Reeled Silk are smooth, flexible & have a sheer texture.

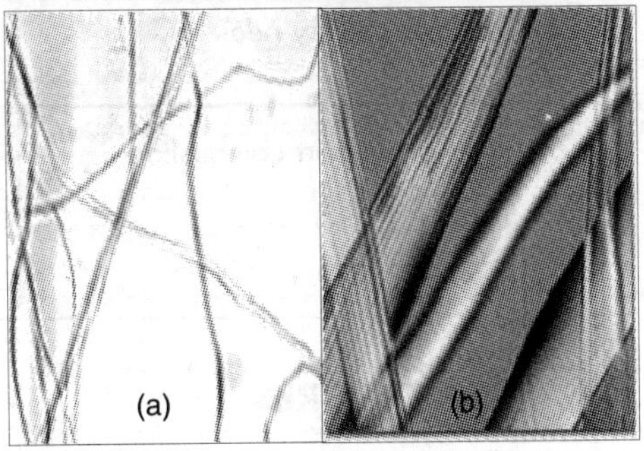

Fig. 4.8 Microscopic view of silk fibre (a) Cultivated silk (b) Wild silk

(b) *Spun Silk*: The short filaments of silk which cannot be reeled are used to prepare spun silk. The fabric thus obtained has a non-uniform appearance and texture.

Fibre Properties:

The microscopic ***longitudinal view*** appears like a smooth transparent rod with many irregular ribbons with scattered gum patches of sericin present.

Cross-sectional view of the silk fibre shows triangular shape with no markings (See Fig. 4.8).

Silk has a good drape, luster and texture. It is primarily used for apparel and furnishing. Silk is extremely versatile and is used to create a variety of fabrics, from sheer chiffons to heavy brocades and velvets including the medium weight crepe. It can be woven as well as knitted. It used to make under-wears, socks, shirts, gowns, upholstery drapes and sheets. It is used in the medical field for sutures and prosthetic arteries.

Basic Properties of Protein Fibres

Properties	***Relative advantages & disadvantages***
1. Resilient	1. Fabrics tend to hold their shape and dont crease readily.
2. Weaker when wet	2. Wool looses about 40% of its strength when wet, Silk about 15%. Must be handled carefully during washing.
3. Harmed by oxidizing agents	3. Chlorine bleaches but damage fibres. Sunlight causes white fabrics to turn yellow.
4. Poor conductors of electricity	4. Provides good insulation and warmth to the body.
5. High absorbency	5. Comfortable in cool, damp climates and absorbs odours.
6. Weakened by alkalis	6. Use neutral or mild soap or detergent. Perspiration weakens the fabric.

Contd...

7. Harmed by dry heat	7. Wool becomes harsh and brittle and scorches easily with dry heat. Silk yellows with high temperatures.
8. Do not support combustion	8. Protein fibres tend to stop burning when the flame is removed. Burned protein fibres have the odour of burning hair or chicken feathers. This test can be used by consumers to distinguish pure wool from acrylic.

MAN MADE FIBRES

Man made are also known as Thermoplastic fibres due to their nature of melting when subjected to heat.

These fibres are composed of synthesized polymers not found in nature but the ones which are chemically synthesized by man. Therefore to have the knowledge about the different manmade fibres, it is necessary to know their raw-materials and manufacturing processes in detail.

Fig. 4.9 A spinerette similar to the shower showing reeling of filaments

Manufacturing process of man made fiber:

Manmade fibres are produced by passing a chemical substance called polymer or dope through a spinerette. This device consists of a series of tiny holes. As the fiber substance solution emerges from the spinerette or is extruded from the spinerette it hardens and coagulates into a fine filament (Refer Fig. 4.9).

The manufacturing process of all manmade fibres is very similar. But there are certain variables that affect the final output of the filament.

(i) The shape of filaments may very depending upon the different shapes of the holes of the spinerette. viz. circular, dog-bone shape, star shape, polygonal etc. This change in shape also tends to give varied cross-sections to the filaments.

(ii) The size of the filament, i.e. finer or thicker depends upon the size of the holes of the spinerette.

(iii) The other variable that affects the property of the extruded filament is the type of environment it is extruded i.e. either it falls into a liquid or hot air chamber or in a coagulating bath. (This process is explained later in this chapter)

(iv) The amount of pressure applied while passing the polymer solution through the spinerette tends to give texturization effect to the filaments.

(v) The colouring pigment and delusturing agents (titanium dioxide) could be added to change the final output of the filament.

Let us take a brief look at some of the important manmade fibres.

NYLON:

Nylon was the first introduced to the world in 1938 by Dupont.

Production of Nylon

Production of Nylon is very simple. Polymer Hexamethyle Diamine and Adipic acid are reacted together to produce Nylon salt. This is then melted and passed through the spinerette to produce Nylon filament.

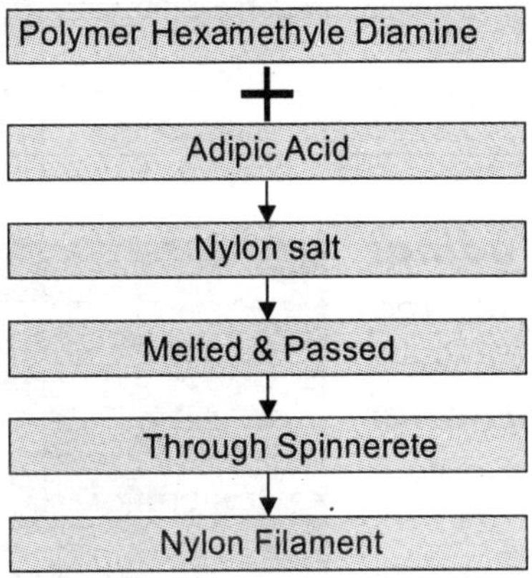

The microscopic view of ***longitudinal section*** of nylon is uniform, glass rod like structure with presence of pigments.

Its ***cross-sectional view*** is trilobal in nature (Refer Fig. 4.10).

Nylon is a popular fabric for apparel and home furnishings. Due to its wash and wear properties and easy care procedures, good dimensional stability and resiliency it is widely used to manufacture, lingerie socks, swimwear, leotards, wind breakers and carpets, draperies upholstery etc. It is also blended with other natural and manmade fibres to provide added advantages of its properties, for varied end uses in industrial and other textile applications.

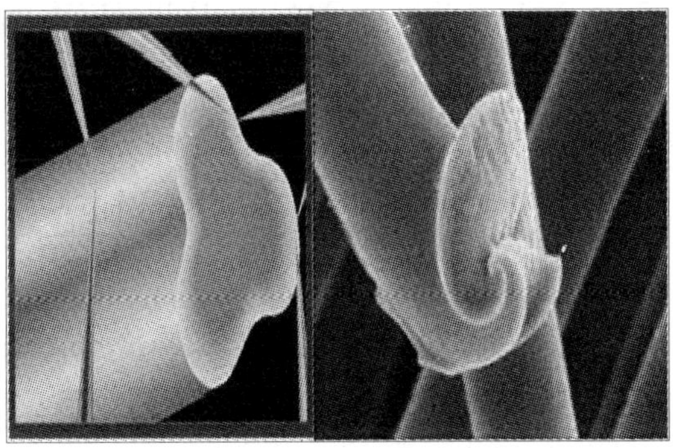

Fig. 4.10 Microscopic view of Nylon fibre

POLYESTER

The first polyester fibre, terylene was produced in England. It was first introduced in the United States by the Dupont under the name Dacron.

Production of polyester:

Polyester is produced by reacting dicarboxylic acid with dihydric alcohol. It is melted and passed through the spinerette and retains the shape of the hole of the spinerette. Change in shape of spinerette hole changes the cross-sectional view of the filament.

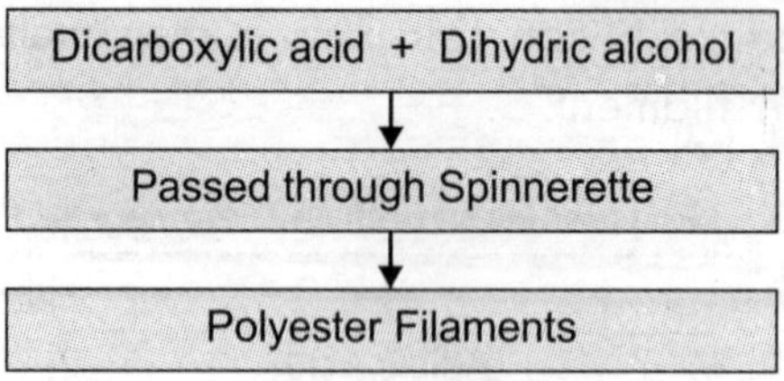

The microscopic ***longitudinal view*** of polyester shows a glass rod like structure with presence of pigments and striations. The ***cross-sectional view*** of polyester is circular in nature (Refer Fig. 4.11).

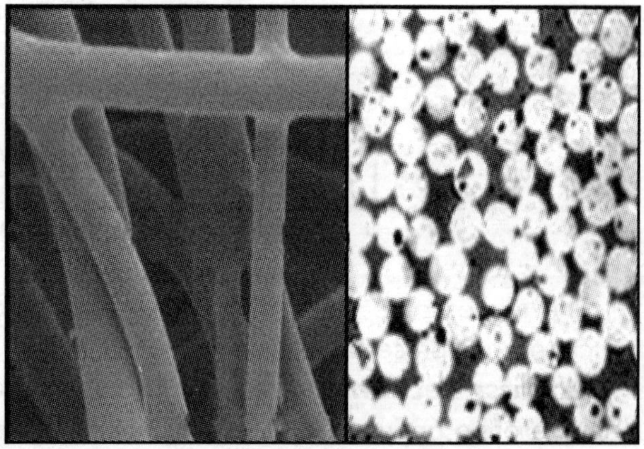

Fig. 4.11 A microscopic view of polyester fiber

Polyester is widely used as a blend or otherwise in woven fabrics used for apparel and furnishings. Polyester kints well and is used for making knitted shirts and blouses. Polyester is used as a fiberfill (polyfill) in pillows, quilts and padding, it is light weight and washable as compared to a cotton filling has gained a lot of popularity. Non-woven polyester is used for making bandages and pads in the medical field.

Polyester is easy to care as it can be washed through dip-dry method. Hot water (120 – 140^0 F) causes wrinkling on the fabric. Polyester is olephilic, i.e. tends to attract oily soils making the fabric look dingy over a period of use. Since they are not absorbent, they are not much comfortable to wear, especially in summers.

ACRYLIC

Acrylonitrile, the substance from which acrylic is made, was first found in Germany in 1893. The marketing of acrylic fibres frequently takes advantage because of its wool like characteristics. It has been given the trademark, "Orlon" by Dupont.

Production: Acrylic fibers are formed by polymerization of acrylonitrile (vinyl cyanide). Solvents dissolve the polymer and then extruded through the spinerette.

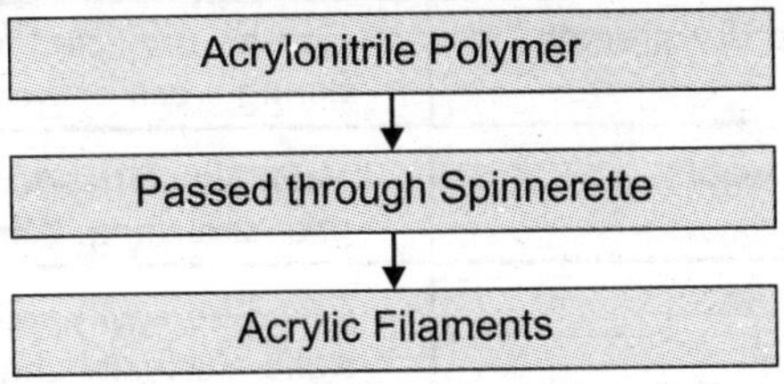

The microscopic ***longitudinal view*** of acrylic shows glass rod structure with irregular presence of striations (Fig. 4.12) and pigments whereas the ***cross-sectional*** is irregular in form.

Fig. 4.12 A microscopic view of acrylic fibre

Acrylic fibres are soft, warm light weight and resilient, they make easy care fabric and are often referred to as "warmth without weight". They are superior to wool in care and storage procedure. Acrylic is used for making furs, socks, coats, jackets and soft stuffed animals. Very often it is blended with wool to make blankets. Pure acrylic blankets and carpets are lightweight, warm and washable and cost less than wool. In the industry acrylic is used to make tents, awnings, bags and office dividers. It is also widely used for upholstery, draperies in the furnishing industry.

Many other recent manmade fibres introduced through various researchers carried out by different textile institutes. These comprise of fibres like acetate, olefin, spandex, lyocell, azlon, acetate saran, vinyl and many more. These fibres are not much popular with the consumers but they have serious applications like for e.g. olefin is a geo textile fibre, modacrylic fibres are used for fire retardant and protective clothings. Other common– uses include sports wear, construction elastic yarns, action wear, moulded garments, printer's blankets, lining fabrics, upholstery, drapery, outdoor furniture etc.

Basic Features Common Man Made Fibres

Property	***Relative advantages and disadvantages***
Wet strength is comparable to dry strength	Can be subjected to agitation or abrasion during wash or wear.
Elasticity and elongation like wool	Maintains air space for warmth. Regains shape after stretching. Affects stiffness, drape, resiliency.
Low moisture absorption	Could be easily washed and dried but builds up static electricity charges and is difficult to dye.
High tensile strength and abrasion resistance	High durability to pulling and rubbing in wear.
High chemical resistance	Resistant to acids, alkalis, bleaches, detergents. Non-hazardous, skin irritant.
Heat sensitive	Melts with (1) hot iron (2) hot tobacco ashes (3) Contact with any hot object.
Can be subjected to Heat-setting	Therefore, Crush resistant pile, Permanent pleats, Embossed designs can be created.
Resilient	Loses wrinkles easily.
High resistance to moth, mildew, insects,	Simplifies storage problems.

REGENERATED MAN MADE CELLULOSIC FIBRES

These fibres are produced by combination of natural, raw materials processed with various chemicals; through different man made procedures. Hence termed as regenerated man made cellulosic fibres.

RAYON

Rayon was the first regenerated cellulosic fiber. It is also called 'artificial silk.

Regular rayon is called viscose rayon. Some rayon is made by using the cupramonium process and is called the cupra rayon under the trade name Bemberg.

Viscose Rayon:

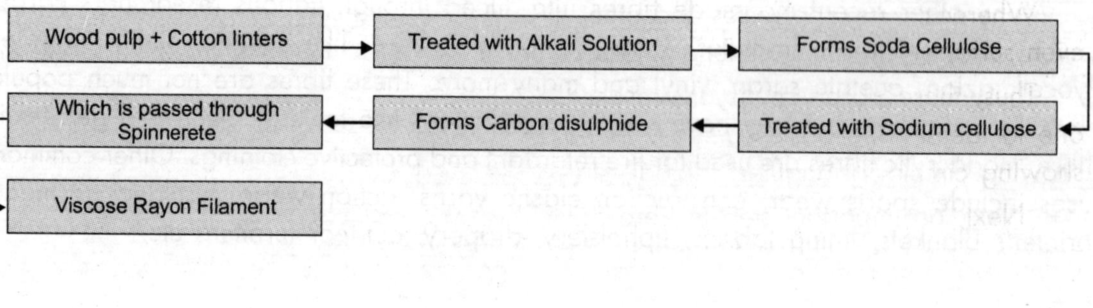

The principle raw material for viscose rayon is wood pulp. Cotton linters are the fibres of cotton that are too short to be spun into the yarn, are also used. These are treated with alkaline solution which results in soda cellulose. This soda cellulose is then reacted with sodium cellulose which produces carbon disulphide as polymer solution; which is then passed through the spinerette to manufacture viscose rayon filaments.

The microscopic view of ***longitudinal section*** show regular rod structure with striations present.

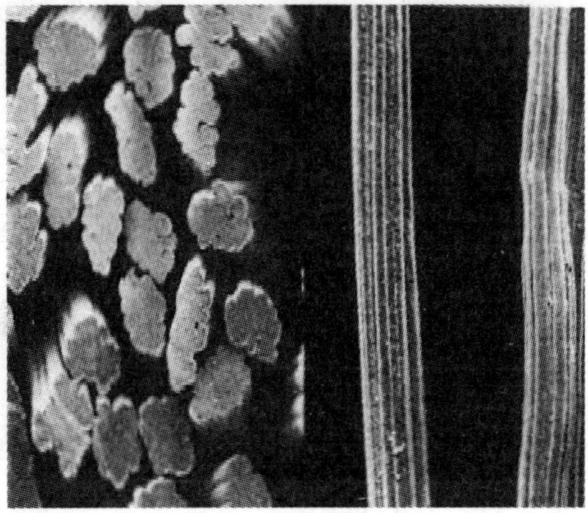

Fig. 4.13 Microscopic view of viscose rayon fibre.

The ***cross-sectional view*** is multi-lobal in nature (See Fig. 4.13).

Rayon is used in woven fabrics especially for apparel and furnishings. It is also used in non-woven fabrics where absorbency is important as industrial wipes, bandages, diapers and sanitary napkins.

Rayon has a low wet strength thus care should be taken while washing. Since it has lusture and texture similar to silk, it is blended with silk to make cheaper version of silk sarees.

The development of new fibres and the modification of the existing ones make the identification of textile fibres more difficult. With common fibres, the identification becomes easy because of the diverse physical and chemical properties and the appearance of the fibres. Therefore, there are 3 methods prescribed by technologists to lead to identification of unknown fibers.

The microscopic test (*longitudinal view and cross-sectional view*) provide a first step of identifying the fibres.

When we study the microscopic test properties of different fibres, the wool is more rough and curly than any other textile fibres, having small scales. Cotton shows ribbon like structure, while bast fibres have striations and uneven structure.

Whereas nylon, polyester and other synthetic fibres have a smooth, uniform and an even surface throughout its length as they are manufactured under controlled conditions.

Thus, these observations of presence of pigments, striations, ribbons, patches helps one to identify the basic category of fibres. In similar manner, the cross-sectional view showing circular, triangular, trilobal, star-shaped views also lead to certain conclusions.

Next, an important step in fibre identification is the ***Burning or Ignition test***.

Vegetable fibres, composed mainly of cellulose, burn readily when ignited and they leave very little or no ash. The burning of cellulose produces odour of a burning paper. Animal fibres have a nitrogenous chemical structure and burn with difficulty, but give out a characteristic odour, which is the one produced when hair or feather is burnt. The fibre leaves a charred globular residue.

Different synthetic fibres behave differently towards a flame, with respect to the rate of burning and to the shape and nature of the ash they leave behind after burning, usually leaving a uncrushable bead as residue with a pungent odour.

Burn Test of Fibres

Fibre	Smell	Ember and Flame
Cotton	Burning Paper	Flame ember or yellow, slow burning; fluffy grayish ash.
Wool	Burning Hair	Small flickering flame, brittle ash, no smoldering (will not burn after flame is removed).
Silk	Burning Feathers	Calm flame, no smoldering. (will not burn after flame is removed). Black beads, crushable.
Nylon	Boiling green vegetables (string beans or celery)	Dissolves and forms an effervescent flame; produces a hard, ember-beaded ash.
Polyester	Sweetish	Burns rapidly; produces a black, hard, rounded ash.
Acrylic	Sharp, pungent, unpleasant odour	Hard, black residue. Burns quickly.
Viscose Rayon	Burning Wood	Rapid burning flame, slow burning embers, no ash, no bead.

Different fibres dissolve in various solvents and this property may also be used to identify them. The difference between the animal and vegetable fibers is more marked chemically than physically. Vegetable fibres withstand the action of alkalis but are destroyed by acids, while opposite is the case with animal fibre.

These ***solubility/chemical tests*** are the confirmatory tests alongwith the microscope test. They are very useful in fibre identification, location of the fibres in mixture and also the quality of different fibres in blends, by dissolving out each component of a particular fibre.

The Chemical Tests of Some Main Fibres

Fibres	**Chemicals**	**Result**
Cotton and Linen	Iodine, 70% Sulphuric acid	Practical dissolution, blue colour completely dissolves cotton
Silk and wool	5% Caustic Soda Picric acid	Completely dissolves wool Permanent yellow colour
Rayons	70% Sulphuric acid, Sodium Zincate	Will completely dissolve
Acetate	Acetone	Will completely dissolve
Nylon	90% Phenol	Will completely dissolve

After we have learnt about the production, processes and physical properties of fibres, we now need to know the next step that is the preparation of yarns from the fibres.

CHAPTER 5

YARN STRUCTURE

HISTORY AND DEFINITION

In simplest term, Yarn is number of fibres twisted or turned together along its length. To weave or knit a fabric it is necessary to have a continuous fibre length i.e. a thread or a yarn .Thus, construction of yarn dates back since the manufacturing of fabric. Primitive people discovered that a succession of short fibres could be twisted into a continuous strand called yarn **(Refer plate 2.7)**. In the beginning the yarns were spun by man with bare hands without the aid of any tools, before the spindle was evolved for spinning (Fig. 5.1).

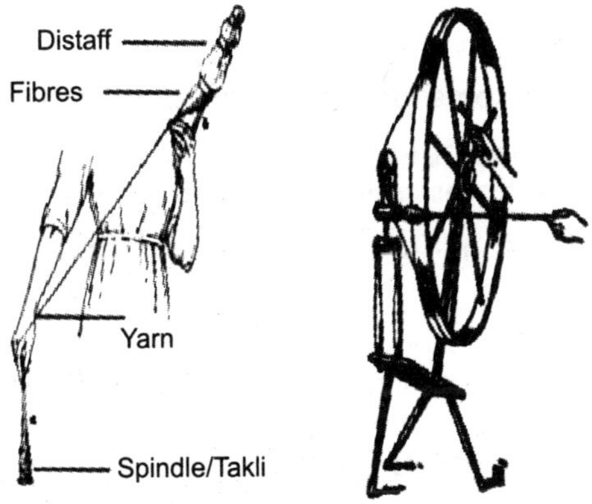

Primitive method of spinning   Charkha spinning

Fig. 5.1 Spinning process

Thereafter "Charkha" was fabricated in India used for spinning a yarn in handloom industry. Now, in textile industries we have electric driven machines employed for spinning i.e. Flyer, Mule, Cap, and Ring spinning systems.

What is Yarn?

A generic term for continuous strands of textile fibres or filaments in a form suitable for knitting, weaving or otherwise intertwining to form a textile fabric. It may comprise of:

(a) A number of fibres twisted together

(b) A number of filaments laid together without a twist (0-twist yarn)

(c) A number of filaments laid together with more or less twist (multi filament)

(d) A single filament with or without twist (mono filament)

Further, The term yarn has been defined by American Society of Testing Materials (ASTM) as:

> *"A continuous strand of textile fibres, filaments, or material in a form suitable for knitting, weaving or otherwise interlacing to make a textile fabric."*

YARN CONSTRUCTION

As defined a yarn is a strand of fibres twisted together by a process called spinning. There are basically two spinning methods.

(i) Mechanical spinning for staple fibres. (especially for natural fibres)

(ii) Chemical spinning for filaments. (man made fibres)

MECHANICAL SPINNING

Mechanical spinning which is carried out especially for natural fibres, (i.e. wool and cotton but not silk), require some pre-spinning operations to form a workable strand as in case of short fibres. The pre-spinning operations are opening, picking, carding and combing. Thus, manmade fibres have a greater advantage at the very beginning when they arrive at the mill to be spun into a yarn as they are of long lengths and free from contaminants and dirt.

Mechanical spinning involves manufacture of yarns from staple fibres. These spun yarns are manufactured by cotton or wool spinning system.

Steps in Mechanical Spinning

Since, the production of cotton yarn lends itself to a simple description of manufacturing operations that make staple fibre into yarn, cotton fibre has been used in this chapter, to illustrate the spinning process.

Summary of the Spinning Process

	Process	Purpose
1.	Opening	Loosens, blends and fluffs the fibre.
2.	Picking	Loosens, cleans, and forms fibre into "lap"
3.	Carding	Straightens fibres and forms the card sliver.
4.	Combing	Straightens fibres, removes short fibres and forms comb sliver
5.	Drawing	Parallels, blends and reduces the size of strands.
6.	Roving	Reduces the size further with a slight twist.
7.	Spinning	Twist and winds the final yarn.

These steps are illustrated in Fig 5.2.

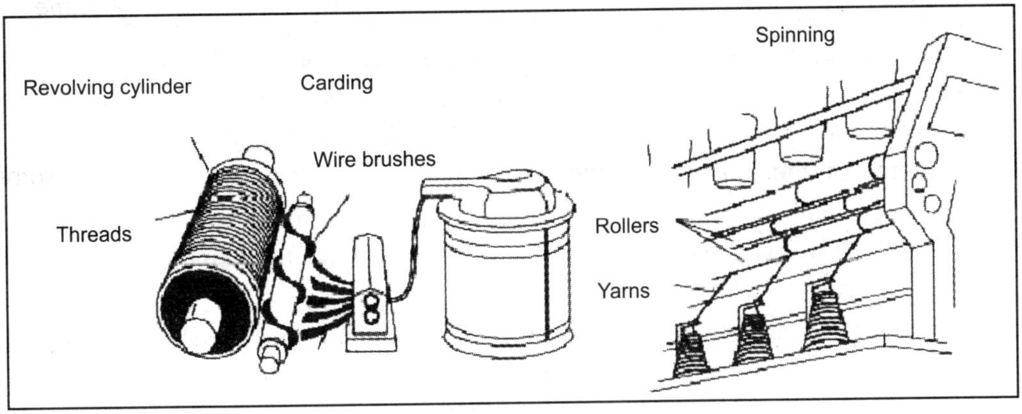

Fig. 5.2 Carding process of cotton

1. **Opening** is the loosening and fluffing of the fibres which have been tightly packed into bales. (A bale consists of fibres of similar length and weighs approx. 500 pounds). Layers of fibre from several bales are fed into an opener at the same time. The fibres emerge from the opener in an immense fluffy mass that is ten to fifteen times as bulky as it was in the bale. The fibres are then blown through tubes to a storage bin where they are conditioned until they reach higher moisture content.
2. The **Picking** machine continues the loosening and cleaning of the fibres and forms them into a continuous thick white sheet called "lap", which resembles absorbent cotton in form and shape. "Lap" a compressed sheet of randomly oriented fibres which is 45 inches wide and 18 inches in diameter.

3. In **Carding,** the fibre lap passes between two cylinders covered with card clothing, which is a heavy fabric embedded with many specially bent wires. Individual fibres are straightened and made somewhat parallel. There is no sorting of long and short fibres. The fibres emerge from the carding rolls as a thin, uniform web which is drawn in a funnel shaped device, where it is gathered into a soft mass and formed into a "card silver", a rope like strand of fibres about ¾ –1 inch in diameter.
4. **Combing** removes the short fibres and places the rest more nearly parallel. Usually one-fourth of the fibre may be combed out as waste, which is used for some other purpose. The "comb silver" now formed is of the fibres that are uniform in length and of a longer average staple. Only long staple good quality fibres are combed. It is an expensive process and adds considerably to the cost of the fabric. Combed fibre fabrics are better, because of the fineness, strength, uniformity, smoothness and luster of the yarns.
5. In the **Drawing** operation several slivers are fed into the drawing rolls at the same time. This is a continuation of the blending, started in the opening process. The drawing frame consists of four sets of rolls, each of which travels at a faster speed than the previous set. The difference in speed causes the elongation of the sliver and draws it into a new sliver (without twist), almost of the same diameter of the original single sliver.
6. **Roving** is similar to drawing since rollers draw out the sliver and further reduce it in size. However, the roving machine puts a slight twist and winds the roving on a bobbin.
7. **Spinning** is a continuous process, with simultaneous twisting and winding operations. The roving passes between rolls which once more draw out the fibres to form a smaller strand. They then pass through a traveler to a spindle which revolves and puts in, an exact number of twists, as the yarn is wound up on a bobbin.
8. **Winding** is the final operation in which the yarn is wound from the bobbins to spools or cones ready for the weaving mills. Some yarns may be wound directly on the warp beams thus saving one operation of the weaving process.

CHEMICAL SPINNING

For manufacturing yarns from all man made fibres, chemical spinning process is employed. The raw materials are treated chemically, and in some cases melted by heating to form a viscous liquid, which is then extruded through very fine holes in a nozzle, called spinneret, and the filaments produced are solidified in various ways.

Basically, there are three different methods of spinning man made fibres.

(i) Wet spinning: The solidification of filaments takes place in the liquid bath.

(ii) Dry spinning: Here, hot and dry air is responsible for solidification of filaments.

(iii) Melt spinning: The filaments are obtained by melting the chips which are then pumped into the spinning chamber (Fig. 5.3).

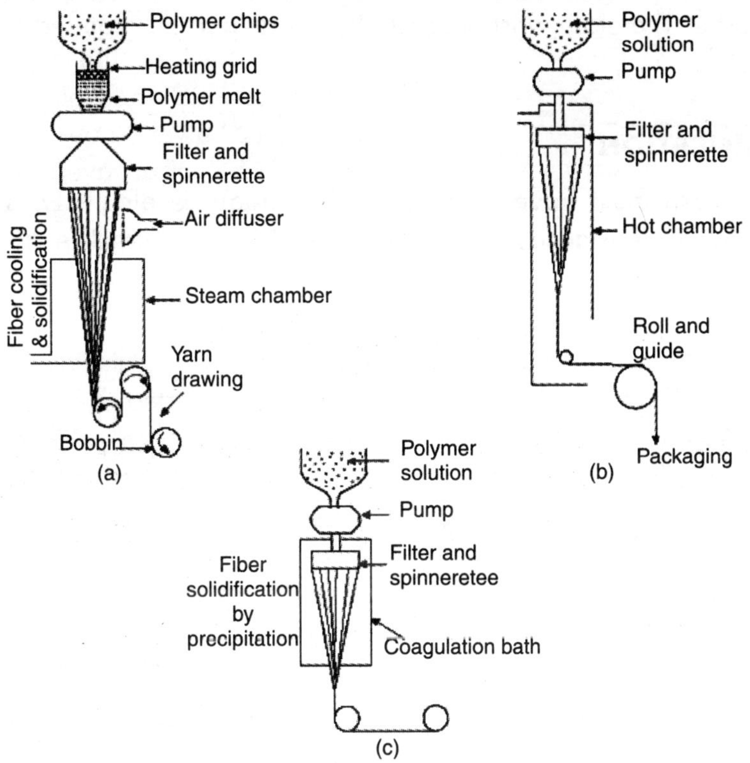

Fig. 5.3 Chemical spinning process (a) Melt spinning (b) Dry spinning (c) Wet spinning

Yarn Twist

Twists are spiral turns given along the length of the yarn. Yarns are twisted either to the right (Z – twist) or to the left (S – twist). The amount of twist is measured by the number of twist per inch (t.p.i.).

The direction of twist is important. Yarns may be twisted either with a right-hand or a left-hand twist. The right-hand twist is called a "Z" twist, while the left-hand twist is an "S" twist. The direction of the twist conforms to the center bar of the letter (Refer Fig. 5.4).

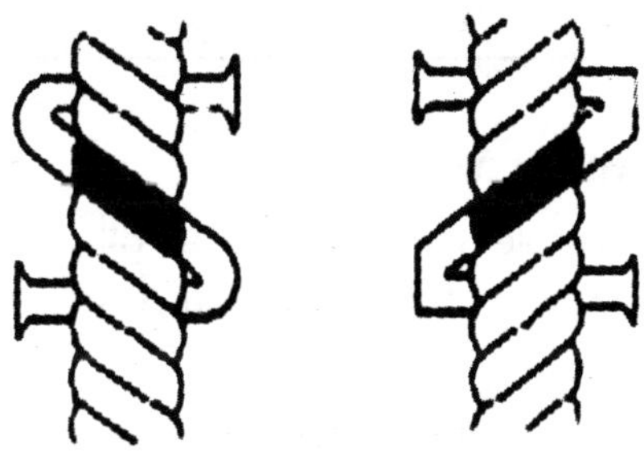

Fig. 5.4 S & Z twist in a yarn

The amount of twist depends on the size of the yarn, the use to which it will be put and the length of fibres from which it is made. Fine yarns require more twist than the coarse yarns.

The amount of twist in a yarn determines many of the characteristics. As a yarn is twisted, it shortens and takes on potential strength. High twist in crepes and georgettes produces much shortening of the yarns and gives possibilities of much stretch. High twist also reduces lustre. Therefore twist needs to be set as per the required parameters in the yarn.

YARN CLASSIFICATION

A satisfactory yarn must have high strength, adequate elasticity, smooth surface, dimensional stability, resistance to damage by friction and attractive appearance. Yarns can be classified as:

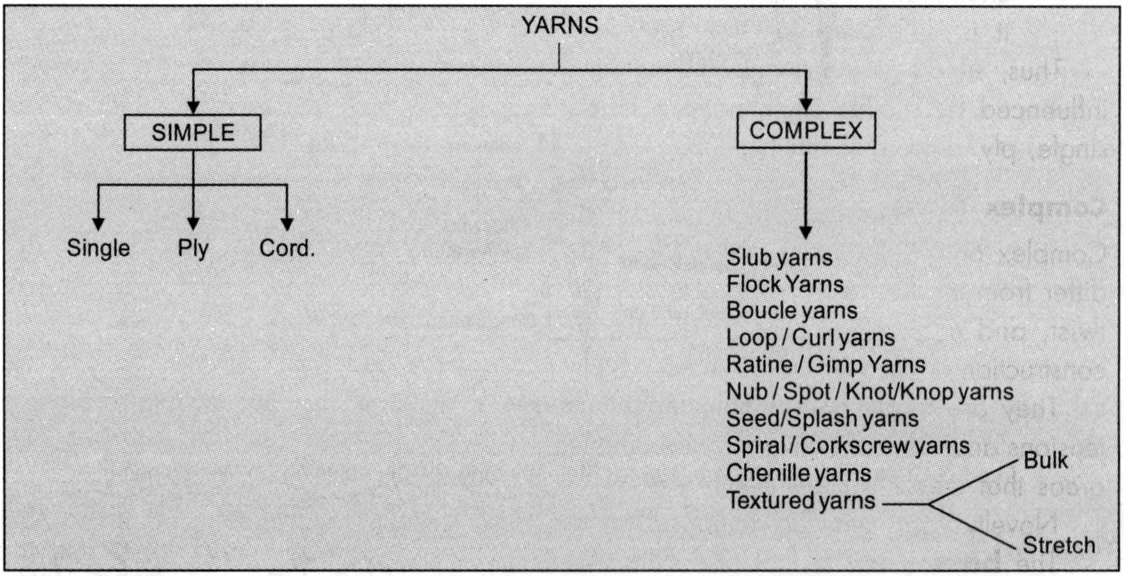

Simple Yarns:

A simple yarn is alike in all its parts, is even in size, have equal number of turns/inch and is relatively smooth throughout, which further constitutes of (a) Single Yarn (b) Ply Yarn (c) Cord Yarn.

(a) Single Yarn is a strand of fibres all twisted in same direction.

(b) Ply Yarn is formed by twisted two or more single yarns together usually with a twist opposite that used in singles. A ply yarn is stronger than single yarn. In naming a ply yarn the number of singles usually precedes the word, "Ply".

For example if two singles are used, it would be called a 2 ply, if there were three singles used, a 3 ply yarn.

(c) Cord yarn : Simple cord or cable yarn is composed of two or more ply yarns twisted together. In identifying a cord it is necessary to indicate the number of plies in the cord for example A "3,5,-ply cord" indicates that each ply has five singles and that 3 of these 5 ply yarns are combined in the making of the cord yarn. These are used in extra heavy industrial fabrics, example, heavy belting material for conveyor, automobile tyre and as contrast it is also used for fine sheer materials.

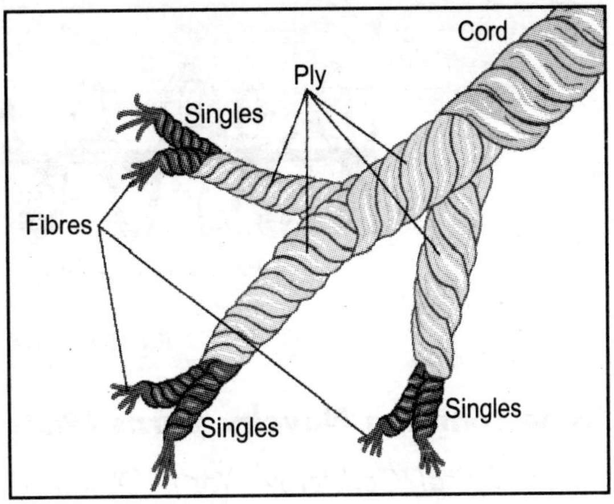

Fig. 5.5 Types of yarns

Thus, simple yarns are usually considered to be durable, although the durability is influenced by factors such as yarn number, amount of twist and whether the yarn is single, ply, or cord (Refer Fig. 5.5).

Complex Yarns:

Complex or novelty yarns are made primarily for their appearance value. These yarns differ from the simple yarns in that the structure is characterized by irregularities in size, twist, and effect. Complex yarns may be single or ply. Occasionally modified cord construction is used in complicated novelty yarns.

They are made on spinning machines with special attachments for giving different tensions and rates of delivery to the different ply, to allow loose, curled, twisted or looped areas that create pattern in the yarn.

Novelty yarns may be composed of the base, the effect, and the tie yarns.

The **base yarn** is that part which controls the length and the stability of the end product.

The **effect yarn** determines and forms the design by the way in which it is applied to the base yarn.

The **tie yarn** is used to attach securely the effect yarn so it will remain in position during use and care (Refer Fig. 5.6).

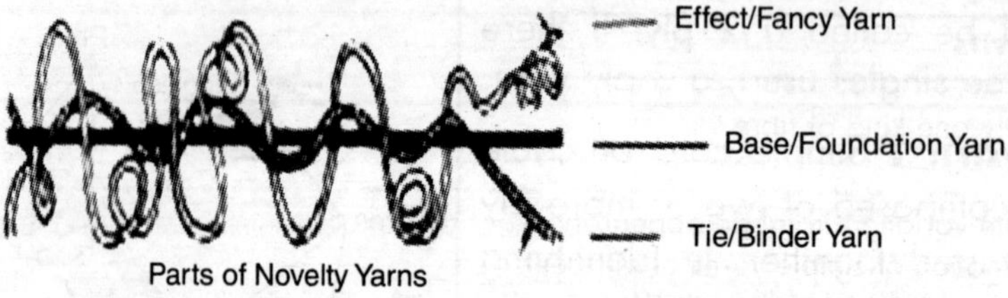

Fig. 5.6 Parts of a novelty yarns.

Some common Novelty yarns (Plate 2.8)

(i) *Spiral/Corkscrew Yarn:* Obtained by twisting yarns of different diameter and different contents at varying rates of speed and direction of twist.

(ii) *Ratine/Gimp Yarns:* Loops are formed close together having a rough surface appearance.

(iii) *Knot/Spot Yarns:* The base yarn is stationary and effect yarn is wrapped around it several times to build up an enlarged segment.

(iv) *Slub Yarns:* Composed of single, 2 ply or more ply yarns which creates softness and bulk due to slack twist at regular intervals.

(v) *Loop/Curl Yarns:* Loops or curls formed around a coarse and heavy base yarns. These are larger and more open. For illustrations of these novelty yarns refer Fig. 5.7 and 5.8.

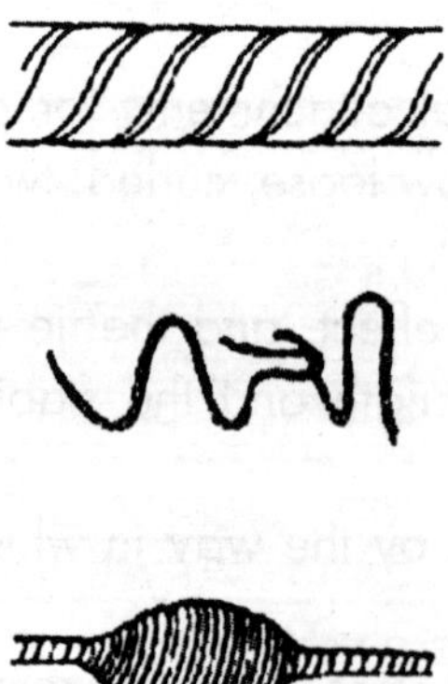

Fig. 5.7 Spiral yarns, Ratine yarns, knot/spot yarn

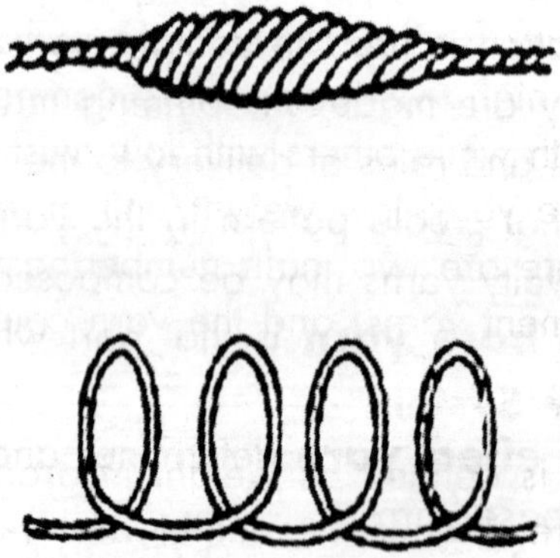

Fig. 5.8 Slub yarn, loop/curl yarn

Difference between Simple and Complex Yarn

Simple Yarns	Complex Yarns
1. Made of only one kind of fibre.	1. Usually constructed of ply yarns of different kinds of fibres.
2. Do not create variation in fabric appearance but a combination of simple yarns of different sizes, amount of twists and fibre contents can produce many interesting effects.	2. Used primarily to achieve appearance value by creating a 3-D effect. They add texture and design to the fabric, make it more interesting with irregular surface appearance.
3. These are more uniform yarns, therefore prevents snagging and tearing.	3. Less uniformity in yarns because of irregular twists and loops cause them to snag easily.
4. More durable, but with respect to different factors like yarn number, amount of twist and yarn structure.	4. Complex yarns tend to have problems in comfort maintenance and durability due to irregular twist and their rough and harsh texture.
5. Used mainly for apparels, and for fabrics where design is applied through colour and finishes.	5. Used for drapery, upholstery and other articles which require design and textural effects.

YARN NUMBERING SYSTEM

Yarns are marketed (bought and sold) by the weight. Yarn numbering systems are therefore used to express a relationship between *a unit length* and *weight* of yarns. The relationship between unit length and weight also reflects the *diameter or thickness* of a yarn. This is so because a yarn of low weight per unit of length would be finer than a yarn with a higher weight per equal unit of length. However, the diameter of the yarn may vary for any given yarn number because of the twist the yarn possesses. Yarns having high twist being more compact, would be thinner for a particular weight per unit of length while others with low twist or which is loose spun has much less twist. In short, finer the yarn, low weight/unit of length coarser the yarn, high weight/unit of length.

There are two main numbering systems in use; the denier system, which is used for all filament yarns, and the yarn count system, which is used for all spun yarns.

Denier System

Denier is defined as weight in grams of 9000 meters of yarn. This means, that thicker the yarn, higher the denier and vice-versa. Very fine yarns of 10 denier are used in sheer hosiery. The heavy, coarse yarns used in carpeting are in cloth range of 2000 denier. The denier system is called a direct system because higher denier numbers designate heavier (thicker) yarn. A, 1 denier yarn is a yarn where 9000 meters, if weighted, would equal 1 gram. A, 2 denier yarn would weight 2 grams for 9000 meters, and so forth.

Yarn Count System

Count is defined as the number of hanks weighing one pound, where the length of each hank is equal to 840 yards.

This means, that finer the yarn, higher the count and vice-versa.

In the yarn count system, the yarn count number is inversely proportional to weight. This system, therefore, is indirect. A 50-count spun yarn has twice the weight (thickness) of a 100-count spun yarn. The weight of the yarn is indirectly proportional to the yarn count number. Cotton yarn, for example, which is used for sheer voile fabrics may be as fine as 100 count, while thicker yarns used in many poplin fabrics may be a 30 count. Heavy cotton duck fabric used for truck tarpaulins may be made of 5-count yarn.

Thus, by having knowledge of the various structures and technical details about the yarns, it facilitates the weavers, and even the designers to manufacture varied fabrics for different end uses as per the demand and requirement.

CHAPTER 6

FABRIC CONSTRUCTION

INTRODUCTION

A textile fabric is the term used for all kinds of cloth having a pliable structure made from fibres or fine filaments by different methods of fabric construction viz. felting, knitting or weaving. The modern textile industry however, has included metal, glass, soyabean, milk etc. under textile fibre which by nature are not fibrous. These non-fibrous material, by the application of certain scientific processes, are converted into fine filaments, which are woven or knitted and these are then included under textile fabrics.

Thus, fabric construction is basically carried out by:

(i) Interlocking of fibres (Felting)

(ii) Interlooping of fibres (Knitting)

(iii) Interlacing of fibres or yarns. (Weaving)

Thus, there are various methods having their relative advantages and disadvantages and accordingly fabrics are constructed as per their end uses.

Felting

It is the massing and flattening or matting together (interlocking) of many fibres by application of heat, pressure, steam or chemicals.

Felting is possible only with the fibres which can stick to one another firmly when pressure is applied and thus, form a cloth.

Example: Felted wool. Wool has a natural tendency to felt which is due to the peculiar construction of the fibre i.e. scales, with or without blending with animal, vegetable or synthetic fibres. **(Refer Plate 2.9)**

Knitting: The fabric produced by this method uses only one thread for its construction. A fabric is formed by a succession of loops, (interloping) i.e. a yarn is wound round a needle to form loops stitches which form one row and then each row of loops interlock with one below it till a continuous length of cloth is made. **(Refer Plate 2.10)**.

The vertical columns of stitches in a knitted fabric are called Wales while Horizontal rows of stitches are known as Courses.

Weaving: The most important method of forming fabrics by mechanical means is weaving. Weaving was used by man for making baskets, mats roofs and walls of huts from the leaves, bark or skin of trees long before he thought of using it for making cloth.

Weaving is the interlacing of two sets of yarn i.e. warp—the lengthwise yarn and weft the widthwise yarn at right angles by means of a loom **(Refer Plate 2.11)**. Before moving to much details of weaving procedures we will understand, the certain basic terminologies of the fabric.

(i) *Selvedge:* The woven edges of the fabric which do not ravel and is parallel to the vertical direction i.e. the grain is the selvedge.

(ii) *Grain:* Refers to direction of threads in a woven fabric. A pattern can be placed on grain or off-grain depending upon the requirement.

(iii) *On-grain:* When grain line on the pattern is matched with the grain of the fabric is said to be on grain.

(iv) *Off-grain:* Any direction in the fabric which does not exactly follow the warp or weft yarn (Refer Fig. 6.1).

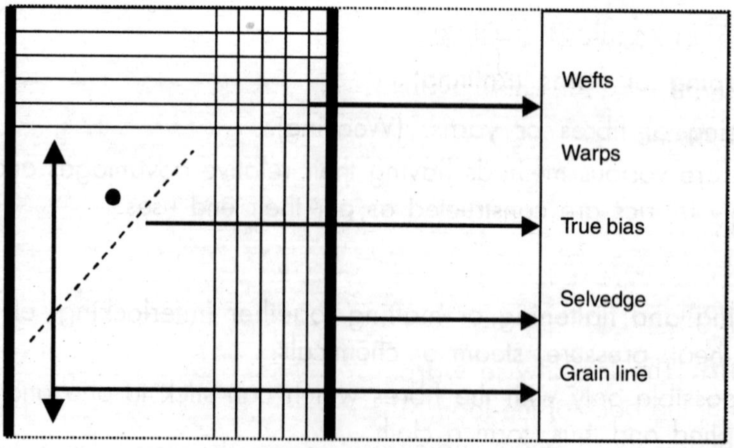

Fig. 6.1 Parameters in a fabric

Lengthwise yarns have minimum stretch, maximum shrinkage and are the strongest yarns since they from the base of fabric. Therefore a fabric should always be cut along the length wise grain to achieve better fit, fall/drape and sturdiness.

Widthwise yarns have more stretch than lengthwise yarns while the bais, at a 45^0 angle has the maximum stretch and best drape. Different patterns of interlacing can give different surface effects or patterns on the fabric.

LOOM AND ITS PARTS

The machinery used for weaving of fabric is known as loom which can be operated by hand, foot or power. (Refer Fig. 6.2).

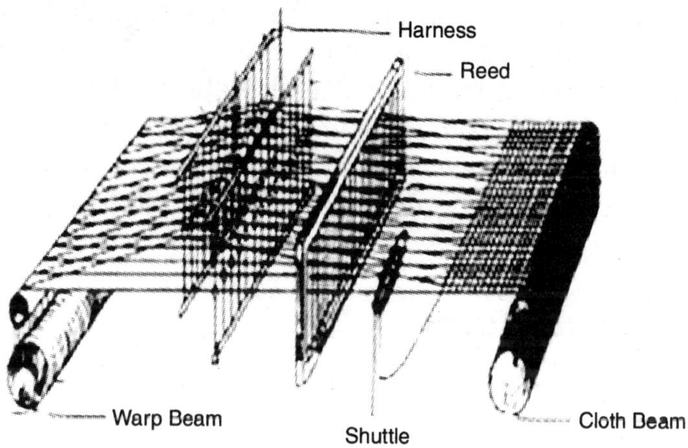

Parts of a Loom

Fig. 6.2

The principal parts of loom, whether it is worked by hand or by power, are the same.

1. Warp Beam
2. Harness Frame
3. Heddles
4. Reed
5. Shuttle
6. Cloth Beam

Warp Beam: The lengthwise warps are wound on the bobbin/beam/cylinder which is located at the back of the loom. These warp yarns are wrapped in parallel lines and the width of the warp beam indicates maximum possible width of the finished fabric.

Harness Frame/Shaft: This frame consists of a number of wires known as heddles. The harness is an important part of the loom as it controls the movement of the warp yarn, upwards (rising) or downwards (lowering) in order to produce a gap/shed for the passage of the weft yarn. Each loom has at least two harness frames. Raising and lowering of the harness in a particular repeat produces the desired pattern in the cloth. Example : In simple plain weave, the movement of the harness frame is 1 up and 1 down which means raising of all warp yarns with the odd number and lowering of all warp yarns with an even number i.e., 1, 3, 5, 7 ... are raised and 2, 4, 6, 8 ..... are lowered to form shed/gap.

Heddle: It is wire or a metal strip with an eye located in the center through which one or more warp yarns are threaded/passed **(Refer Plate 2.11(a))**.

Reed: It is a comb like device which keeps the warps separated. The space between each wire in the reed is called a dent. This helps in packing the weft into position. It also helps in maintaining the width of the fabric **(Refer Plate 2.12)**.

Shuttle: It is a device which carries the weft thread that is wound on a bobbin. The shuttle is thrown/passed from one end to the other through the shed **(Refer Plate 2.13)**.

Cloth beam: It is cylinder/beam/bobbin located at the front of the loom. It holds finished fabric under tension.

BASIC STEPS IN WEAVING LOOM

1. *Shedding:* It means raising and lowering of the warp yarn by means of a harness frame into two layers, one top and one bottom, so as to form a passage for the shuttle to travel across the warps; first forwards and then backwards along the width of the fabric to be formed. The opening/passage that is formed is called a "shed".
2. *Picking:* It refers to the insertion of weft/filling/picks by the shuttle moving through the shed across the warp yarns.
3. *Beating:* It is the process of beating or forcing the weft yarns against the previous filling; firmly in position by means of a reed or batten and the process is also known as battening.

Types of Looms

(a) Shuttle Loom (b) Shuttle-less Loom

(a) Shuttle-Loom: This is a conventional loom which utilizes a shuttle that contains a bobbin of filling yarn, which emerges through a hole in the side. As the shuttle is batted across the loom it leaves a trail of the filling at the rate of about 110 to 225 picks per minute (ppm).

The shuttle loom is the oldest kind of loom. It is effective and versatile but it has certain disadvantages. The shuttle sometimes causes abrasion on the warp yarns as it passes over them and sometimes causes thread breaks. This, in turn, results in machine stoppage in order to tie the broken yarns. Shuttle looms operate more slowly than some new types of looms and, they are also noisier. **(Refer Plate 2.14)**

(b) *Shuttle-less Looms:* To overcome disadvantages of the shuttle loom, different kinds of shuttle-less looms have been developed. Each type uses a different method of picking, i.e. passing the weft yarns, which provides specific characteristics and applications. These are classified as under:

- (i) Missile or Projectile Looms
- (ii) Rapier Looms
- (iii) Water-jet Looms
- (iv) Air-jet Loom

These looms use a metal/composite bar or rapier or water or air pressure to pass the weft yarn from one end to another instead of conventional shuttles.

Researches are being carried out all over the world to design and derive loom which could further facilitate the quality and speed of weaving.

Types of Weaves:

The manner in which groups of warp yarns are raised by harness to permit the insertion of weft yarn determines the pattern of the weave. Weaves are in accordance with the design followed in interlacing these yarns. The basic/fundamental weaves used in fabric construction are:

1. Plain weave
2. Twill weave — Also, known as ABC Weaves **(Refer Plate 2.15)**
3. Satin weave

These are the foundation weaves and form the basis of all the other types of weave patterns. For example, Double cloth, lappet weave, Dobby, jacquard, or triaxial weaves, leno weave are called combination or derivative weaves. These combination weaves are also known as pattern/figured/novelty weaves since they provide interesting surface effects having decorative designs or textured surface.

Thus, multicolour effects with unlimited ranges of intricate designs could be woven with the help of the combinations or decorative weaves. Plain weave is a basic style of all the weaves.

Plain Weave: It is the most common of all the weave construction. This weave resembles the process of darning or basting. It consists of alternate interlacing of warp and weft yarns along the entire width of the fabric, i.e., the weft yarn moves/passes over one warp and under the next warp yarn and so on. This is denoted as 1 up 1 down or 1/1 interlacement **(Refer Plate 2.16)**.

The simplest loom for plain weave has two harnesses/shafts. The plain weave is also known as Homespun cotton, Taffeta or Tabby Weave, which produces a checkerboard effect.

Features of plain weave:

- It is the most inexpensive/cheap weave.
- It has great utility because of its texture and appearance (which is uninteresting) and is made interesting by printing, embossing etc.
- It provides a wide scope for introduction variation in the fabrics, such as the use of yarns of different colours, different fibres, different twists etc. *Example:* Seersucker, Flannel, Gingham.
- It has no wrong side due to its construction i.e., distinguishing between the right and the wrong side is difficult.
- It is the most serviceable of all weaves, as fabrics with these weaves are easy to maintain and care.
- Also, they seldom ravel because of greater number of interlacement.

Examples of some plain weave fabrics are cambric, voile, muslin, chiffon, flannel, crepe, georgette, casement, etc. **(Refer Plate 2.17, 2.18 and 2.19)**.

The classification of plain weave is as follows:

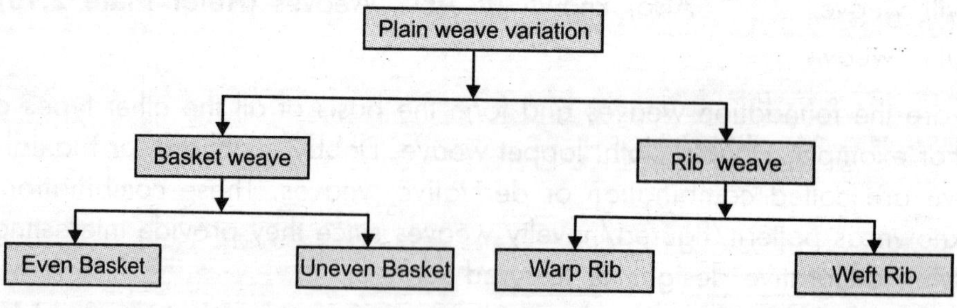

These variations make plain weave fabrics appear more attractive.

Basket Weave: In this two more yarns in both warp and weft are treated as one, and interlaced as in plain weaves. The woven pattern consists of 2 up 2 down (2/2) 3 up 3 down (3/3) so on.

Basket weave is typically used in composites industry & used as Metti cloth/monk's cloth and draping fabrics **(Refer Plate 2.20)**.

Basket weave is a balanced weave. If it is not compactly woven (low fabric count) then the fabric is porous and pliable. This weave is used in materials for sport coats and suits. Since, it is comparatively a loose weave, the fabrics therefore are more likely to shrink and are not suitable for hard wear.

Rib Weave: This is a basic weave pattern which is characterized by prominent rib pattern in warp or weft directions **(Refer Plate 2.21, 2.22)**.

Rib effect is produced in the warp or in the weft by alternating fine yarns with coarse yarns or single yarns with double yarns. i.e. if warp yarns are coarse and weft yarns used are fine which produces the ribbed effect. Example – Poplin

Ribs may be lengthwise or widthwise. The interlacement pattern remains the same i.e., 1/1 the main difference lies in the thickness of yarns used in warp and weft. When rib weave has a two yarns grouped to form one, it has greater abrasion resistance and tear strength.

Twill Weave: This weave forms wales diagonally across the face of the fabric. This distinct design in the form of diagonals is the characteristic feature of twill weave. The diagonal effect is brought about by interlacing of warp and weft yarns with a progression of one at the point of interlacing. This progression may be to the right or to the left. It may be plain or varied which makes the cloth decorative. The weave requires at least three shafts or the harness. In the twill weave, weft yarn interlaces more than one warp yarn but never more than four warp yarns. The interlacement pattern therefore, would be 1 up 2 down, 1 up 3 down or 1 up 4 down **(Refer Plate 2.23)**.

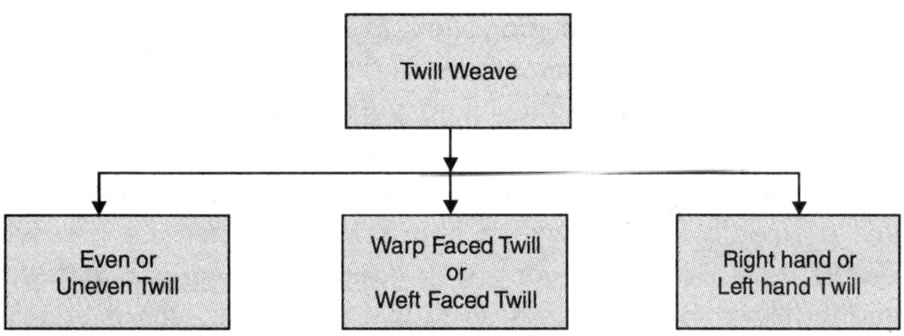

Even or Uneven Twill: It refers to the interlacement being even or uneven example 2/2 interlacement is even and 1/2, 1/3, 2/1 etc., are uneven.

Warp Faced or Weft Faced Twill: It refers to the yarns which form the face of the cloth, i.e. when the warps form the wales it is warp faced and when the weft yarns are seen more on the face of the fabric forming the wales it is weft faced twill.

Right Hand or Left Hand Twill: It refers to the direction of the wales. In a right hand twill the diagonals extend from lower left to the upper right hand corner and in the left hand twill the diagonals extend from upper left to the lower right hand direction of the cloth **(Refer Plate 2.24 and 2.25)**.

Features of Twill Weave

- Twill weave has fewer points of interlacings than plain weave.
- The fabrics made by twill weave are generally closer in texture than plain weave. Thus, they are heavier in weight and more stronger.
- Twill weave fabrics are more expensive because of their elaborate construction.
- The fabrics made are more durable and stand hard and long wear. Hence, it is preferred for men's outer clothing.
- Also, they do not show dirt or dust as much as fabrics in plain weave do.
- The diagonally arranged interlacing provides greater pliability and resiliency.

Example of some Twill Weave Fabrics are Drill, Denim, Jeans, Khakhi, Flannel etc.

Twill Weave Variation: Variations in the twill weave are introduced by changing the direction of wales example, Herring bone. Also, by using yarns of different sizes, qualities and colours, effects can be introduced.

Satin Weave: Stain weave is a more flexible type of weave than plain weave but it is more complicated.

In basic construction satin weave is same as twill weave but differs from twill weave in appearance because the diagonals of satin are not visible. It is purposely interrupted to contribute to a flat, smooth and lustrous surface. Here, the interlacing of warp and weft yarns is irregular. The filling yarns passes under several warp yarns thus throwing up the warps on the surface of the cloth and the wefts on the inside or wrong side of the cloth. The exposed warps or weft are called floats. The long warp floats produce a smooth surface with a characteristic luster, i.e. the warp faced is known as "***Satin***" and weft faced (long weft floats) is known as "***Sateen***" weave. In sateen weave the filling yarn is thrown up to the surface i.e., the interlacing would be 4 up and 1 down, 4/1 which means the weft passes over four warp yarns and under one warp and this interlacing obviously would give weft floats on the surface and the interlacement for satin weave would be opposite i.e., 1/4. The interlacing float may have interlacing like 4/1, 7/1, or 11/1 **(Refer Plate 2.26)**.

A satin or sateen weave generally employs five to thirteen harnesses. Apart, from the direction of float deciding the kind (satin or sateen) of weave, we generally have shorter floats in sateen as compared to satin.

Features of Satin Weave

- Fabric made from such weave are much more expensive than the twill or cotton since these require more shafts or harnesses.
- Short float fabric is more durable than the long, but they do not have luster or brilliance, i.e., longer the float, less durable the fabric.
- Long floats are subject to damage from abrasion or rubbing.
- They generally shed dirt well, but spots and stains are as visible as smudges on a mirror.
- These weaves are more decorative than serviceable i.e., they cannot be put to hard use.
- This weave is most commonly used in the silks and rayons and thus, they are extremely lustrous and smooth. This makes them a better choice for materials used as coat linings since they can be slipped on and off with much ease.
- This weave is also occasionally used in mercerized cotton fabric. They are not as smooth or lustrous as satin and are often woven with the sateen weave, example: upholstery fabrics. Example of some fabrics with satin and sateen weave are brocade, crepe, damask. Tie fabrics, sateens, etc. **(Refer Plate 2.27).**

Satin Weave Variation

Sateen weave is a variation of satin weave. The other variation may be introduced by using different qualities of yarn such as tightly or loosely twisted yarns or by throwing long and short floats upon the surface. A combination of satin and sateen weaves may be used to produce elaborate or figured weaves. Thus, in the stain weave, the float is in warp directions whereas as in sateen, it is in weft direction **(Refer Plate 2.28)**.

Now let us study in short the 2 main figured & decorative weave formulation, amongst many mentioned above:

Dobby weave: Small figured designs, which require less than 25 different yarn arrangements to complete one repeat of the design, are made on a loom with a dobby attachment usually referred to as a dobby loom **(Refer Plate 2.29)**.

Two methods are used to create a pattern, in the older method the weave pattern is controlled by a plastic tape with punched holes. The holes control the position of each warp yarn in forming a shed. The newer method creating simple geometrical pattern in the fabric uses a computer to control the position of the warp yarns. This system is faster and allows for easy and quick pattern changes in the fabric.

Many designs made on tape of dobby loom are small geometrical figures. Dobbies may be of any weight or compactness, with yarns ranging from very fine to coarse and fluffy. Standard dobby fabrics are usually flat and relatively fine or sheer. Some heavy weight dobby fabrics are available for home furnishings and for heavy apparel. Some examples are shirting madras, waffle cloth, brocades, dish and bar cloths, upholstery and apparel, diamonds or dot at centre **(Refer Plate 2.30)**.

Jacquard weave: Large-figured designs, which require more than 25 different arrangements of the warp yarns to complete one repeat design, are woven on a jacquard loom **(Refer Plate 2.31)**.

Two types of loom are used to produce jacquard weaves. In the older types of loom, each warp is controlled independently by punched cards that are laced together in a continuous strip. The position of the warp yarn is controlled by rods, attached to them. When the rod hit the cards, some go through the holes raise the warp yarns other remain down. Thus, a shed is formed for the passage of the filling yarn. The newer method for producing those large patterns in the fabric uses a computer, often designed to be used with an air-jet loom and referred to as an electronic jacquard. This system is very fast and allows for easy and quick pattern changes.

Fabrics produced on a jacquard loom include damask, brocade, tapestry and a variety of other patterns **(Refer Plate 2.32)**.

IDENTIFYING THE WARP AND WEFT YARNS OF FABRICS

It is important to identify the warp and the weft yarns of fabrics before cutting them, because fabrics for garment construction are often cut on a straight grain. The procedure of identifying the yarns may appear very simple, as the warp yarns are always parallel to the selvedge. But at times, one might have to create garments from fabric pieces which do not have the selvedge. It is here one needs to determine the warp and weft yarns and in turn the selvedge/grain. The following points aid the determination of the respective yarns.

When weave of the fabric is known

- The greater number of yarns running in one direction, in plain weaves indicates the warp.
- In satin weave, the floats are comprised of the warp yarns. When the fabric is examined by touching, the finger will slide in one direction, which is the warp.
- In sateen weaves, the floats are comprised of the filling yarns. When the fabric is examined by touching, the finger will slide in one direction, which is the weft.

When weave of the fabric is not known

- Hold the piece of sample in hand and pull it, at the same time pressing with the thumb and fore fingers, the yarns which sustain the tension are usually the stronger yarns and the warp yarns.
- The yarns which have a hard twist are generally the warp yarns. For testing this, strands of yarn have to be unraveled from both sides of the fabric and untwisted.
- If sample contains one set of thicker yarns, it is usually the weft yarns.
- Yarns which are more easily stretched are the weft yarns.
- If inferior yarns are present, they are usually the weft yarns.

IDENTIFYING THE RIGHT AND WRONG SIDE OF FABRICS

Identifying the right side of fabrics is important before they are applied to any use. Usually the right side of fabrics are lustrous than the reverse side, for printed fabric the designs appear more prominent on the face side. However, it is also important to determine the right and wrong side of woven materials.

- *Plain weave:* Usually the knots and defects present in the plain woven fabric are placed on the wrong side of the fabric.
- *Twill weave fabrics:* The right side of twill fabric has document ridges and hollows to identify a twill line.
- *Satin weave fabric:* The right side of the fabrics are more lustrous than wrong side. The weave floats are longer on right side.

After, the basic study of fibres, yarns and fabrics, it is important to know that how creative combination of these could result in producing more serviceable and durable and economical fabrics through their mixing and blending.

MIXTURES AND BLENDED FABRICS

Until the end of the last century the natural fibres were the only ones available. Combination of fibres in fabrics had warp yarn made of one type of fibre and filling yarns of another. With advent of manmade fibres, two or more fibres are combined in one fabric. Blends and mixtures are successfully used in all types of fabrics so as to make them suitable for varied end uses like under-garments, sweaters, bushshirts, suits, drapery fabrics, blankets, work clothing, rain-wear, children's wear, sports wear, etc.

Although the terms 'mixtures' and 'blends' are commonly inter-changed, technically there is a difference in their meaning.

Mixture Fabrics are those made up of two or more different kinds of yarns, each of which is composed of only one kind of fibre. The yarns may be composed of filament or staple length fibres. For e.g. A mixture fabric may have polyster as wrap yarns and cotton as weft yarn.

Blended Fabrics are made up of yarns in which two or more different kinds of fibres are spun together. In addition various types of monofilaments or filament yarns may be combined or twisted together to form a 'combination' filament yarn. In a blended fabric, polyster and cotton fibres are combined/spun together as a yarn and then fabric woven is a blended polyester/cotton fabric.

There are several advantages for mixing and blending.

1. They obtain a larger number of desirable characteristics than can be achieved by using one fibre alone such as increased absorbency, comfort, fastness to light, greater resistance to abrasion, wrinkle resistance, strength, elasticity, resiliency, dimensional stability, fabric attractiveness, better texture, drape and softness, reduced tendency to pilling, mildew, bacterial growth and static electricity accumulation, possibilities of creating newer mixtures of colours and designs, permanent pleating, embossing, printing and other special effects. Thus, in short the fabric improves in appearance, behaviour and utility; it becomes cheaper and easier to care for.
2. Cellulosic fibres are often included in the mixtures or blends to give increased washability and greater affinity for dye stuffs and chemicals in finishing. Thermoplastic fibres are used to improve crease resistance, shape retention, abrasion resistance, strength elongation, drying time, ease in ironing, pleating, etc. Rayon and cotton on blends help to keep costs low and to increase absorbency and washability. Nylon serves to improve toughness and abrasion resistance; polyester to improve wrinkle resistance; acetate to improve drape texture and also resistance to wrinkles.

TECHNIQUES AND TECHNOLOGY

Section III

Learning objectives:

By the end of this section, you will get a clear picture of:

- What is a finish and classification of finishes.
- Different finishes and finishing materials required to change the yarn or fabric appearance.
- Basic preliminary steps to finishing viz. scouring, bleaching, calendering etc.
- Application of colour and design on the fabric through dyeing and printing by various types and applications.

CHAPTER 7

INTRODUCTION TO TEXTILE FINISHING

Finishing is the general term for a multiple processes and treatments which a fabric is subjected to, after its construction; either after weaving or knitting or after its surface ornamentation; i.e., after dyeing or printing process. In simpler terms, one can define finish as a process that is done to fibre, yarn or fabric to change its appearance, feel and performance and make it suitable for its intended end use.

When the yarn or fabric comes from the spinner, weaver or knitter, it is in raw condition and always contains impurities which are natural to the fibres. The manufactured textile is in a grey or dirty brownish colour such materials are often referred to as being in the grey or brown state. Thus, they are in a very unattractive stage, which requires a careful choice of surface processes and conditions for successful finishing. The group of finishings that are used for many types of fabrics include scouring and bleaching, dyeing, printing, singeing, tentering, calendering, sanforising, mercerizing, schrienerising, moireing, weighting, embossing, etc. These finishes may be applied in combination with, or before or after, manufacture so that they acquire an attractive appearance and improve their serviceability in many ways.

Textile finishes and finishing are classified in several ways. First classification is on the basis of aesthetics and functionality. The designers who are concerned with usually the final look of their end product categorize the finishes as ***aesthetic finishes*** while the marketers and merchandisers are involved with trading of fabrics classify finishes by the performance of a fabric under specific end use conditions as ***functional finishes***.

The textile processors and chemists further categorize finishes into ***chemical finishes*** or wet processing finishes where the chemicals are applied to change the appearance, hand or texture.

Finishes are also categorized by their degree of permanence. These finishes are called permanent, durable, semi-durable and temporary.

Permanent finishes usually involve a chemical change in fibre structure and will not change or alter throughout the life of a fabric such as mercerization, lasts the life of the textile substrate.

Durable finishes usually last throughout the life of the article, but effectiveness becomes diminished after each usage and age and subsequently the finish is nearly removed such as wrinkle resistance.

Semi-durable finishes last through several launderings or dry cleaning and many are renewable in home laundering or dry cleaning such as water repellent finishes, can be applied by the consumer or the drycleaner. Temporary finishes are removed or substantially diminished the first time an article is laundered or dry cleaned such as simple Calendering lasts until the item is washed or dry cleaned.

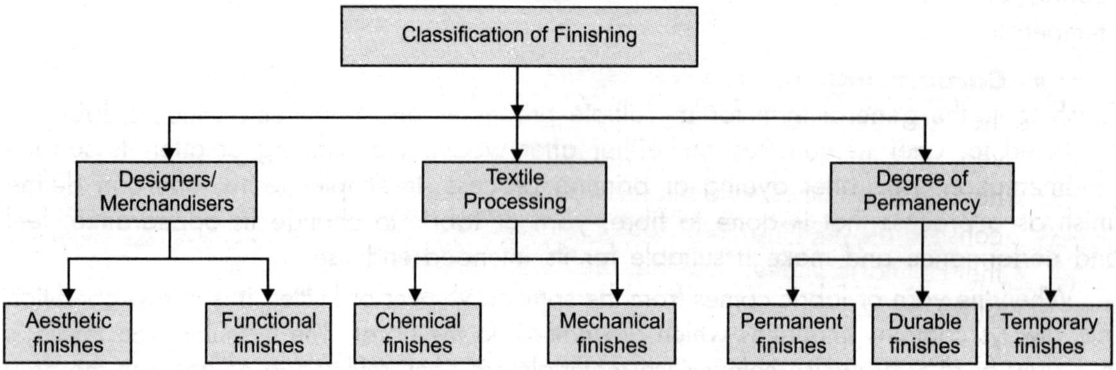

Finishing may be done in the mill where the fabric is produced or it may be done in a separate establishment by a highly specialized group called converters.

PRE-TREATMENT PROCESSES

Before carrying out any procedures of finishing, dyeing or printing certain pre-treatments are required on the fabric which consist of cleaning operations to rid the fabric of the soil and additives that is accumulated during the weaving or knitting process. These processes are usually the first treatments a fabric undergoes after leaving the loom or knitting machine.

- **Scouring/Boil-off:** During the construction and processing the textile goods pick up, oils, waxes, starches and other foreign matter, and impurities, therefore complete removal of these elements is necessary which is done by the process of boil off or scouring in soap solutions at high temperatures. But, since the fibres have different affinity to the various purifying agents, therefore different classes of textile materials should be treated accordingly.

The processes consist of various type of cleaning actions, depending upon the fibre, the impurities present and the fabric construction. In cotton, cotton blend, silk and manmade fibres, the processes are known generally as the boil-off, in woolens and worsteds, it is called a scour or scouring. The machinery required is different according to whether the textile substrate is in form of fibre yarn or a fabric and even in case of fabric, the machinery differs based on whether the fabric is woven or knitted **(Refer Plate 3.1)**. Fabrics may be scoured and bleached in either rope or open width form. Soaps or synthetic detergents with alkaline builders and with wetting agents constitute the most common scouring agents. When this process is used for protein fibers, the chemicals selected should be natural or slightly acidic. The fabric is then treated with the combination of these agents as per the requirement and subjected to high boiling temperatures. This process, thus removes impurities from the textiles at the first stage.

- **Carbonizing:** This is a pre-treatment process that is carried out generally with the woolens and worsted fabrics. Wool yarns and fabrics frequently contain vegetable matter that is not completely removed during carding or it may also have leaf particles and bits of grass or other cellulosic impurities. The treatment consists of steeping the wool fabric in sulphuric acid solution which destroys the cellulosic matter leaving the wool unharmed. Carbonizing is a chemical finish, therefore, the process must be carefully controlled to prevent fiber damage, which would result in weakened fabrics.
- **Singeing:** It consists of burning off the projecting fuzz or fiber ends on fabric in order to obtain a smooth surface. This is one of the important step of pre-treatment processing in which the fabric is passed over a hot plate or through a gas flame at a high speed flame in open-width form at the rate of 230 to 270 yards per minute so that the projecting fibres are burnt and a smooth surface is obtained on the fabric. The fabric after passing on an open gasflame and enters a water bath as soon as it leaves the singeing area **(Refer Plate 3.2)**.

This is a process through which loose fibers, lint, dust and pilling is removed and the surface is made more lustrous but improper singeing or elimination of this operation results in unclear print patterns, mottled fabric surface or premature pilling of fabrics.

- **Desizing:** It is the process of removal of starch from the fabric. After the process of singeing, the fabric is fed into the water bath to eliminate the after glow or the sparks of the flame. At this time it is also saturated with the desizing enzymes in the same water bath, thus also known as desizing bath. Since, most of the yarns are given some type of sizing prior to the placement on a warp beam for weaving, but after fabric is woven the stiffness in the fabric is not required for further finishing treatments. Thus, the presence of these enzymes work on the sizing agents and desize them.

- **Bleaching:** It follows the normal scouring operation during the pre-treatment processes. Bleaches are used to obtain pure whiteness since natural fibres are rarely pure white in their natural state. They are usually slightly yellowish or greyish. During the bleaching process the chemical agents react with colour compounds in the fibre and render them colourless. Usually bleaches like hydrogen peroxide, sodium hypochlorite, or chlorine compounds are used for bleaching silk and wool and all cellulose fibres and rayons. In addition, caustic, wetting agents, detergents, optical brighteners, are included in the bleaching solutions. The reaction of these components removes waxes, foreign matter and any discolouring material present on the fiber, yarn or fabric and thus making the substrate more brighter and whiter. Besides all, sunlight with moisture, air and grass is the oldest, easiest and cheapest method of bleaching. At mill level, yardages of fabric are bleached at a time through mechanized machinery as illustrated in **Plate 3.3**.

Apart, from these general pre-treatments there are certain other important finishes, which include;

Certain finishes which increase or change the aesthetics of the fabric like;

- Calendering
- Single Calendering
- Glaze Calendering
- Embossing Calendering
- Moire Calendering
- Schreiner Calendering
- Mercerization
- Durable Press Finish/Crease Resistance Finish
- Napping
- Plisse

Other finishes which improves the functionality of the fabric such as;

- Shrinkage Control Finishes
- Soil Release Finishes

- Flame Resistance Finishes
- Waterproof Finish/Water Resistant Finish
- Antistatic Finish
- Antiseptic Finish
- Moth Proof Finishes

The application of all these finishing treatments on to the surface any textile substrate is done usually by two basic techniques or machineries which are improvised as per the requirement of the converter.

The padding machine is used to apply dyes and finishing chemicals in either liquid or paste form to the fabric. Padding is done by passing the fabric through the solution, under a guide roll, and between 2 padded rolls. The type of roll depends on the finish to be applied. The rolls exert tons of pressure on the fabric, forcing the finish into the yarn and fabric on both the sides of the fabric (See Fig. 7.1).

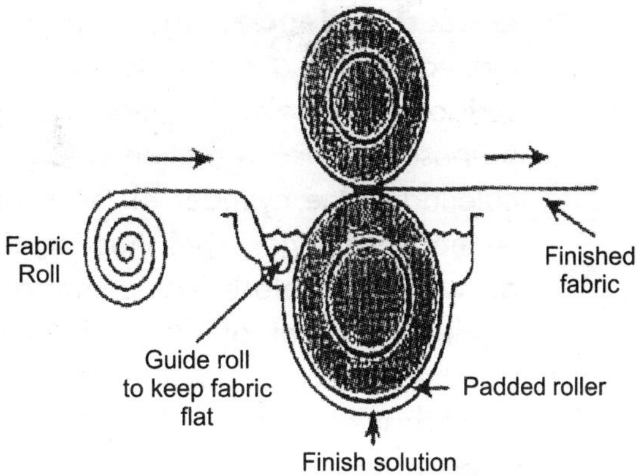

Fig 7.1 Padding machine used in finishing process

The back filling machine is a variation of padding machine. It applies the finish to one side only, usually the back of the fabric (See Fig. 7.2).

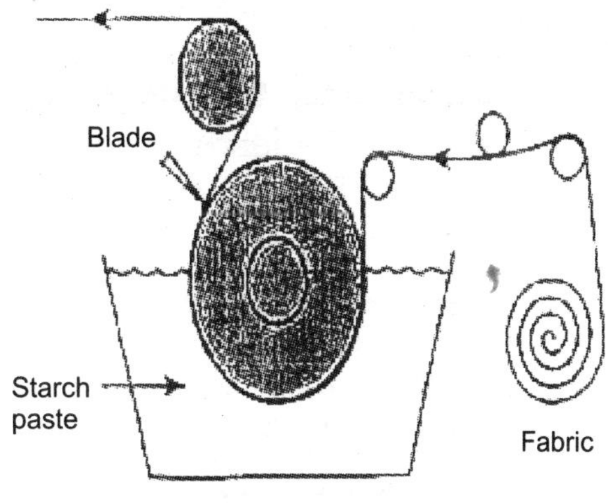

Fig 7.2 Figure of a back-filling mangle for finishing of fabrics

- **Calendering:** It is an important finish that increases the luster and softness of the fabric. It is essentially an ironing process in which the fabric is passed around and between the steam heated cylinders or rollers under high pressure and moisture. Calendering flattens and closes the threads of the fabric to give it the required smooth feel and appearance. The type of finish depends chiefly on pressure, temperature and moisture. This finish aids in ironing of fabric at mass production level and making it wrinkle free. Fabrics like broadcloth, poplin, taffeta and similar materials which appear to be excessively lustrous and soft are calendered.

Simple Calendering is a mechanical and a temporary finish. The flattened yarns in the fabric usually return to their natural round configuration on the first laundering or steaming.

There are various types of calenders, producing different types of finished fabrics, some using friction, and other waxy substances to give added luster and effects. (See Fig. 7.3).

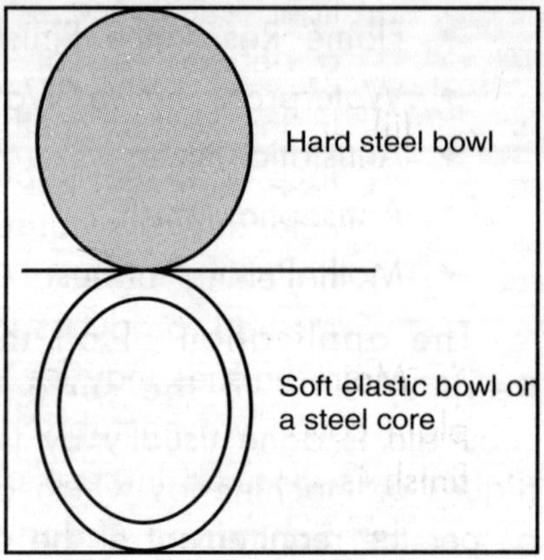

Fig 7.3 A two bowl calender for calendering purpose

- **Glazed Calendering:** It produces a highly glazed, polished effect on one side of a fabric surface. The calendar machine used for this purpose is called a friction calendar or chasing calendar. One cylinder of the friction calendar is made of highly polished steel. The speed at which it rotates is comparatively much higher than that of the fabric as a result, a polished effect is obtained on the surface of the fabric.

In order to obtain this glazed appearance certain pre-treatments like saturating the fabric with solutions of either starch or resins is required. If the pre-treatment is carried out using starch, then the finish obtained is temporary whereas with resins the effect produced is permanent. Polished cotton and chintz are two typical fabrics finished by glazed Calendering.

- **Embossing Calendering:** Embossing produces a three-dimensional design effect on the fabric surface. It is the process of producing raised effect on fabric surface. This effect is obtained by passing the fabric through the resin and then pressing in the design with special embossing calendar which has engraved rollers, that makes the fabric surface raised and depressed at different places. The form of the design that could be chosen may be large or small, floral or geometric and may be of one or more colours. The colour and resin can be added at the same time. The process can be applied to fabrics made of all types of fibres with the exception of wool. This finish is permanent when applied to fabrics made of thermoplastic fibres since the heated metal roll will heat set the fabric design. This finish is temporary on natural fibres and will wash out of fabric unless resins are used to make them durable. Embossed fabrics usually look similar to the dobby or jacquard woven fabrics. **(Refer Plate 3.4)**
- **Moiré Calendering:** A moiré finish produces a wood grain design or a watermarked appearance on the surface of a fabric.

There are two methods for producing moiré.

(i) In the first method, fine lines are engraved on the cylinder roller on the calendar which flattens one part of the fabric more than another causing the different light reflectance, which results in watery moiréd effect. Through this technique, a definite repeat pattern is produced.

(ii) In the second method, two unbalanced plain weave rib fabrics, each face to face, are fed through the calendar. The high pressure of 8–10 tons on the calendar rolls causes the ribs to squeeze into each other in certain areas. This flattening parts of the fabric and creating the light reflectance pattern. This method produces a completely random, non-repetitive moiré.

Moiré finishes may be temporary, durable or permanent. If the moiré is obtained on plain cotton woven fabric the finish is temporary. If the fabric is treated with resin the finish is durable. In case of thermoplastic fibres the moiré finishes are permanent.

- **Schreiner Calendering:** Schreiner Calendering is the opposite of the other calendar finishes. It produces a low luster on the fabric surface in comparison to the high glaze and shine of different calenders. It also produces a softer hand and improved fabric cover. Schreinerzing is an inexpensive method for imparting luster to low-priced cottons. To produce this effect, one of the steel cylinders of the calendar is embossed with very fine diagonal lines, about 250–300 lines per inch. The fabric is then passed between the rollers. Due to the exerted pressure the diagonal ridges are impressed on the fabric surface. Since the reflection of light is obstructed due to these ridges, it imparts luster which is low and soft. Schreiner Calendering may be a permanent, durable or temporary finish similar to the moiré finish. The finish is widely used on nylon tricot, cotton and polyester/cotton sateen and damask table linen and is also suitable for linings and sateens.

- **Fulling:** Fulling is a permanent finish used on wool fabrics; also known as milling. During this process the wool fabrics are subjected to scouring or laundering under controlled conditions. As a result of this process, the fabric shrinks and the resultant fulled fabric is smoother, more compact and has yarns more tightly embedded than an unfulled fabric. The degree of fullness can be also altered as per the thickness and compactness required in the wool fabrics.
- **Napping:** Napping is one of the permanent finish which is used to obtain a relatively deep hairy fabric surface. To facilitate the process of napping, the fabric intended to be used for the process is constructed through yarns which are given a slack of less twist during the spinning process. The fabric is then passed under the roller that has fine steel wires with small hooks on the ends. The hooks scrape the surface of the fabric pulling up fibre ends out of the yarn **(Refer Plate 3.5)**. Thus, the napping process apart form providing textural changes has few other advantages. It produces a softer and thicker fabric which provides insulation and warmth and covers up wearing imperfections, reduces

luster and increases resistance to stains due to pile effect created. But excessive napping tends to weaken the fabric, and has tendency to pill.

- **Plisse:** Plisse is a finishing effect which is obtained through printing. The cotton fabric is printed by sodium hydroxide in form of stripes or some patterns using blocks. As a result the printed or the treated area shrinks due to the reaction between the alkali and the cotton and the untreated area puckers. Also the shrinkage causes the treated fabric area to become compact and denser giving a crinkled effect to the fabric surface. Plisse gives a similar effect of a seersucker fabric; but seersucker is not a finish and is obtained through varied warp tensions during the weaving process **(Refer Plate 3.6)**.
- **Mercerization:** Mercerization is a chemical finish which is permanent and one of the most important of all cotton finishes. It was discovered in 1853 by John Mercer, a calico printer. This finish consists of treating the material with 18 to 20 per cent concentration of an alkali caustic soda for one and half to two minutes at room temperature under tension. As a result, this treatment produces a permanent change in the structure of the fibre, which cause the fibre to swell. Because the fibers are under tension during swelling, they gain a rounder cross-section, and the number of convolutions in the cross section of the fibre decreases. The smoother fibre reflects more light and thus produce a silky luster. Both fabrics and yarns (but not the fibres) can be mercerized. Mercerization is used on cotton, linen, and some rayon fabrics. Besides imparting luster, mercerization increases the strength of the fabric by nearly 25-30%.

  It increases absorbance because the caustic soda causes a rearrangement of the molecules, thus improving moisture regain to approximately 11 per cent. It also improves dye affinity, producing brighter and deeper shades than unmercerized cotton and also utilizing lesser amount of dye stuff than normally required for same depth of shade. It also enhances the hand and softness of the textile substrate.
- **Crease Resistant Finishes:** Crease resistant finishes are popularly known as CRF finishes.

  These finishes are usually applied on natural fibres like cotton, rayon and linen since these fibres tend to wrinkle easily. The crease resistant finishes are durable finishes which are resin treated and may wipe off on regular usage. During the finishing process, the fabric is treated with resin and is cured at temperatures of about 360° F. As a result, the fabric becomes stiffer, less absorbent and more resistant to wrinkling. But these resin treatments also results in loss of tensile strength and reduction of abrasion resistance in cellulosic fibres.

Another similar type of finish in this category is durable press which is not a specific textile finish, but a term synonymous to permanent press used for garments or other sewn products which maintain a pressed appearance through many launderings and usage and do not require ironing.

- **Parchmentizing:** Parchmentizing is a finish that renders transparency to the cotton fabrics. Parchment effects are produced by treatment with sulphuric acid under controlled conditions. Before the process, certain pretreatments like singeing, desizing, bleaching, and mercerization are carried out. Thereafter, the fabric is immersed in the exact concentration of acidic solution for required time period. The acidic reaction partially dissolves the fibre surface and as a result the cellulosic film hardens and the fabric surface becomes crisp and transparent. After the sulphuric acid treatment, the cloth is neutralized through mercerization process and calendared to improve surface gloss. This all over treatment produces transparent and crisp organdy fabric, which could later be dyed or printed for surface ornamentation. **(Refer Plate 3.7)**.

  After, having some general idea about the finishes that improve the surface texture or aesthetics of the fabrics, we will now study about the finishes that improve the serviceability or functionality of the fabric.

- **Shrinkage Control Finishes:** Before having an insight about the shrinkage control finishes we need to understand the reasons and causes that lead to shrinkage of the fabrics.

(i) The textile fabric is made up of threads which are in a state of deformation as they are strained and stretched for the process of interlacing or interlooping with each other during the weaving or knitting process (Refer Fig. 7.4).

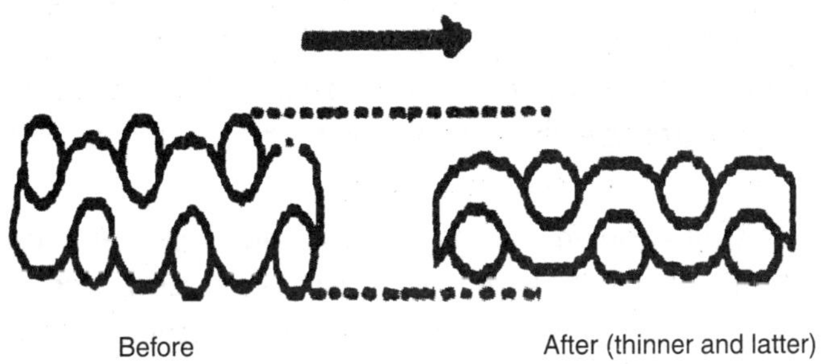

Fig 7.4 Shrinkage process in a fabric

(ii) Fabric design and construction is another factor that leads to shrinkage. If the fabric is openly or loosely constructed or if it has less number of yarns per inch, it will shrink more. Compared to this a compactly constructed fabric having more number of yarns per inch will have less shrinkage, because in the first case there are interspaces in between the yarns which allows the movement of yarns to take place when subjected to launderings. For the same reason, fabrics containing low-twist yarns will tend to shrink more than fabrics with tightly twisted yarns.

(iii) After the construction of the fabric, it undergoes various finishing treatments. When finished, the cloth passed through Calendering or other machines to bring it into a smooth condition, the fabric is further stretched, and will tend to shrink, when laundered.

But it is also important to know a fabric's shrinkage potential because it helps determine how a garment should be designed and constructed. Therefore to adhere to certain parameters of quality and to gain customer satisfaction with regard to fit, the manufacturers provide preshrunk or sanforized fabrics. Sanforising is the processes in which the length of the fabric is contracted or the fabric is made to shrink before its marketing process, by passing it between the seam heated cylinders padded with blanket. As a result of this process he fabric shrinks, and thus aid the consumers.

There are two kinds of shrinkage: relaxation shrinkage and progressive shrinkage.

- **Relaxation Shrinkage:** Relaxation shrinkage occurs only once, when the fabric is subjected to laundering for the first time. The reason for this shrinkage is that during the spinning and weaving process the fibres and yarns are subjected to constant stress and strain of twisting, warping, tieing etc. So, when the fabric becomes wet or steamed in a tensionless condition, the stresses and strains become relaxed and as a result relaxation shrinkage takes place.
- **Progressive Shrinkage:** Progressive shrinkage on the other hand occurs constantly each time the fabric is subjected to the laundering process. Usually fibres like wool (which undergoes felting during laundering) and viscose rayon (which has greater absorbency and swelling features) are prone to progressive shrinkage action. Therefore each time either of these fabrics is laundered the fibres present, rearrange themselves and as result progressive shrinkage takes place.

  As a result of shrinkage the yarns move closer together thus forming a compact fabric structure. This gives more body, increased strength, improve fabric properties like abrasion resistance, greater elasticity and less distortion.
- **Soil Release Finishes:** Soil release finishes, as the name suggests allows easy removal of soils especially oleophilic soils (ones having more attraction to oils) in polyester or resin treated fabrics which have low wetting and low absorbency properties.

There are several types of soil release finishes having one common goal of making the fibre more absorbent (hydrophilic), thus permitting better wettability for improved soil removal. These finishes are durable finishes and usually applied to work clothes, shirts, slacks and table cloths. Apart from increased absorbency, the soil release finishes if applied also tend to provide better drapablity; anistatic and comfort properties.

- **Water Repellent and Water proof Finishes:** Water repellents are durable finishes which repel water. In this finish the yarns but not the fabrics are coated with the water repellent chemical which resists the penetration of water though the fabric, but permit the passage of moisture or air through the interspaces of the yarns. The chemicals used are waxes, emulsions or certain other chemical which allow raindrops and other liquids to remain on the fabric surface in a small bead rather than to spread out and become absorbed. Thus, the water repellent fabrics allow passage of moisture but not the water. But in conditions which require complete protection from water as well as moisture, the fabrics are given water proof finish by the coating or laminating the fabric with a film of natural or synthetic rubber, or plastic, such as vinyl or polyurethane or more recently coated by resin or by teflon.

Even though they provide greater protection, waterproof fabrics are less in demand than water repellent fabrics since they do not have air permeability and thus are uncomfortable, non-pliable, stiff and non-drapable.

- **Anti-Static Finishes:** Anti-static finishes are applied on to the fabric at mill level to eliminate dryness and static electricity from the fabric. Certain chemicals arc applied on the surface of the fabric which have the ability to absorb moisture from the atmosphere, thus reducing dryness and increasing the anti-static properties of the textile fabric. The chemicals used for anti-static treatment are formaldehyde, zinc chloride, calcium and magnesium chloride.
- **Antiseptic Finishes:** Antiseptic finishes are chemical finishes which are applied to the fabric to prevent bacterial growth in textiles and clothing accessories such as shoes luggage, and up to a certain permissible limit on children's clothing to make them germ free. These finishes are low in cost, easily applied and are durable to laundering and dry cleaning.
- **Flame Resistant Finishes:** The anti-flame finishes cannot be made absolutely fire-proof, but they can be chemically treated to be flame resistant. The fabric can be made flame resistant by either using the fibres having flame resistant properties during fabric construction or by applying finishes which have anti- flame properties. These finishes are usually applied on fabrics used in mattresses, work clothes or draperies.

At household level, treatment of the fabric with borax and boric acid also results in fire proof properties.

- **Moth Proof Finishes:** All the natural fibres especially animal fibres like wool are attacked by moths and larvaes. They feed on the fibre and thus form holes in the wool fabrics creating moth eaten or moth affected fabrics which needs to be protected. The moth proof finishes are chemical finishes which are relatively permanent, easy to apply and low in cost. These finishes are applied at the time of dyeing and finishing stage and added in the dye bath. Most commonly used finishes are fluorides, silico fluorides, DDT, Benzene which are fast to dry cleaning, but not fast to washing. Another means of controlling is to change chemically the fibre to make it unpalatable to the larvae. Chemicals causing these changes are added during the dyeing process and are fast both to washing and dry cleaning.

  Finishes; are thus of varied types, applied on different fabrics through different procedures; using special chemicals and solutions in respective concentrations; to achieve the required effect and output as per the need and requirement of the final consumer.

CHAPTER 8

DYEING TEXTILES WITH COLOURS

INTRODUCTION

After the fabric is subjected to various finishing pretreatments and after treatments to improve its aesthetics and functionality the next step is the dyeing of the fabric which is an additional means of enhancing the beauty and appearance of the fabric.

Dyeing is employed to render colour and give solid shades all over the fibre, yarn or fabric. The dye molecules do not stay onto the surface of the fibre but are absorbed into the pores of the material since the shape of the dye molecules is similar to the narrow strips of paper and smaller than the size of the pores in the fibre. This assists the dye molecules to slip into the polymer system and there it is held by forces of attraction when the fibre, yarn or fabric is introduced into the dye bath.

Thus, dyes are organic compounds which are widely used for imparting colour to textiles. They are produced either chemically or from plants and animals.

Up to the middle of nineteenth century, primitive people obtained dyes from flower, nuts, berry, and other forms of vegetable and plant life, as well as from mineral and animal sources. The principal vegetable dyes are catechu, madder, henna saffron, logwood, indigo, and alizarin. Animal dyes, such as cochineal, squid, lac, and tyrian purple, are obtained from species of fish and small insects. Minerals provide such dyes as Prussian blue, chrome yellow, and iron buff. These sources have provided such natural dyes throughout civilization. They are no longer used in quantity by the dyeing industry, but they are still used for rug dyeing and in many parts of the world for traditional handicrafts.

But as these dyes are not simple water-soluble substances, complex procedures were used to provide better and standardized dye colours.

In 1856 a British chemist named William Henry Perkin, produced a brilliant mauve dye stuff from coal-tar which was the first synthetic dyestuff.

The discovery and manufacture of dyes from coal derivatives has today brought at the disposal of the dyer thousands of synthetically made dyes, which are easy to apply and give shades of varying brightness and fastness **(Refer Plate 3.8)**. These dyes can be classified according to their chemical structure or according to their affinities for the different textile fibres. Generally there are special methods or application for each of these different classes of dyes.

Presently the natural dye consumption is equivalent to only 1% of the world synthetic dye consumption. Steps are being taken to revive natural dyes in view of their toxic effects of synthetic dyes on the environment and following a ban on certain synthetic dyes. But this revival would be time taking. We shall focus on the properties of some important classes of synthetic dyes. The classification is based upon the particular type of chemical composition of the dye:

(a) **Direct Dyes:** Direct dyes are also known as 'salt dyes' or cotton colours, which dye cotton, other vegetable fibres and viscose rayon. They are readily soluble in water and are applied to cellulose fibres by adding an auxiliary which is usually sodium chloride as it accelerates the rate at which the dye is picked up by the fibre. These dyes are cheap and easy to apply, but of poor fastness quality.

(b) **Basic Dyes:** The first coal-tar dye was a basic dye applied to wool, silk, cotton and acrylic, fibres. These dyes give brilliant and have good fastness properties. But if these dyes are applied on cotton, mordanting process is pre-requisite for better results of dyeing. Mordants are the intermediary substances like copper, tin, aluminum etc., which help in better fixation and absorption of the dyes.

(c) **Acid Dyes:** These are soluble in water and are applied under acidic conditions usually to protein fibres like wool and silk. The maximum quantity of dye absorbed depends on the amount of sulphuric acid present in the bath, as an auxiliary. Acid dyes are inexpensive dyes and are fast to light, but they are not fast to washing.

(d) **Vat Dyes:** Vat dyes are hot water dyes. They are insoluble in water, but are solublized by agents such as sodium hydrosulphite dissolved in sodium hydroxide. These dyes have excellent fastness properties and are applied usually on cotton, linen, rayon and also to wool, nylon, polyester etc. The first synthetic Vat dye was an *Indigo* created in 1879.

Vat dyes are expensive because of the initial cost as well as the method of application.

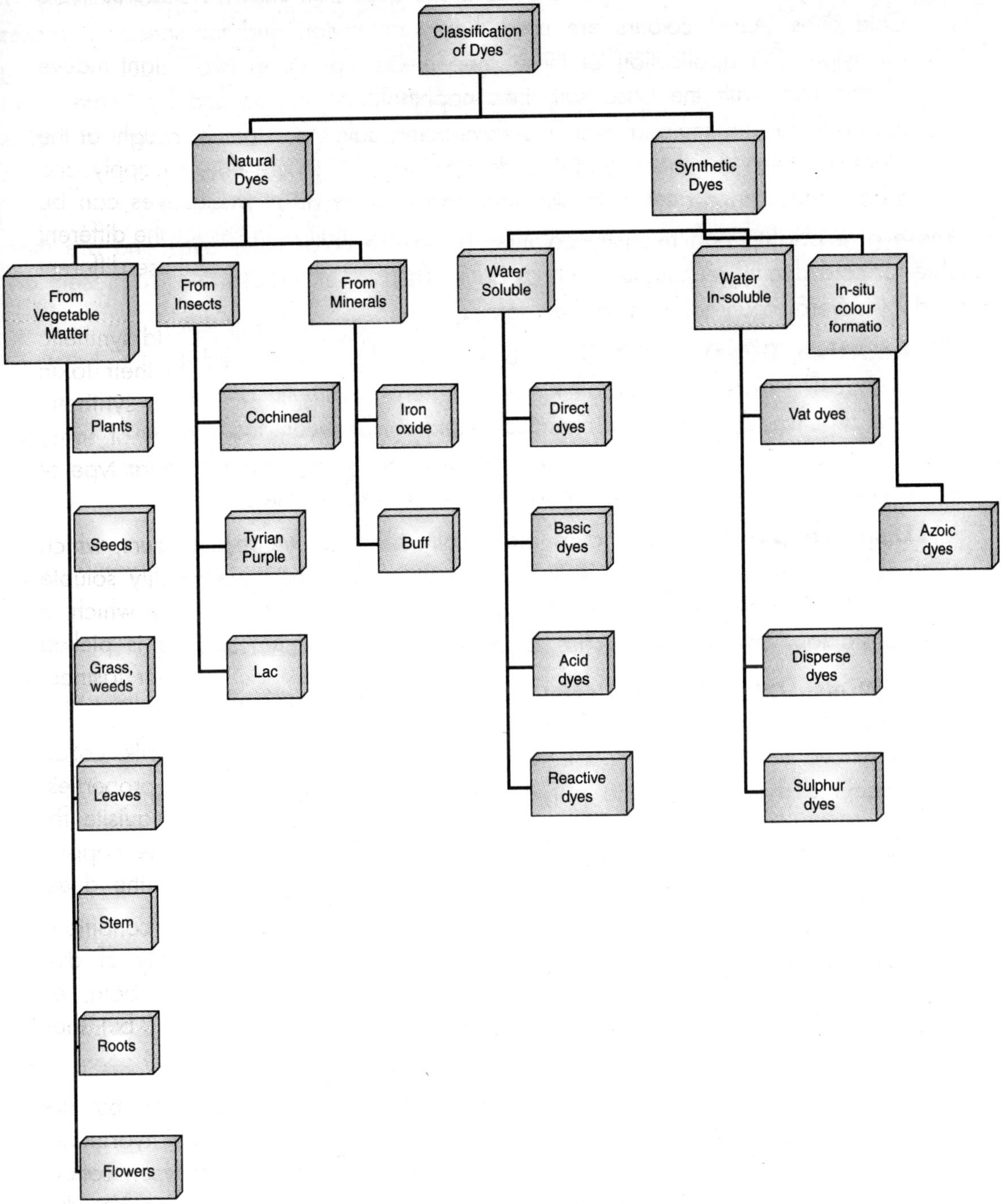
Classification of Dyes
Natural Dyes
Synthetic Dyes
From Vegetable Matter
From Insects
From Minerals
Water Soluble
Water In-soluble
In-situ colour formatio
Plants
Seeds
Grass, weeds
Leaves
Stem
Roots
Flowers
Cochineal
Tyrian Purple
Lac
Iron oxide
Buff
Direct dyes
Basic dyes
Acid dyes
Reactive dyes
Vat dyes
Disperse dyes
Sulphur dyes
Azoic dyes

(e) **Azoic Dyes:** The Azoic dyes are the in-situ dyes also known as Naphthol dyes/ Cold dyes. Azoic colours are used mostly on cotton and for special purposes on nylon. The application of these dyes is carried out in two stages consisting of treatment with the base salt, i.e., naphthol and the second by treatment of the naphtholated material with the developing salt. As a result, a reaction takes place between the base and the developing salt, thus rendering colour to the fabric. They are quite fast to washing and have poor to *excellent* light fastness.

These give bright, high intensity colours. These are cold water dyes and are most suitable for cold dyeing techniques such as Batik, Tie-Dye, etc. These dyes at present are banned by several countries due to their toxicity.

(f) **Reactive Dyes:** The Reactive dyes were first developed by I.C.I , U.K. in1956.They are used for all kinds of natural, synthetic and polyamide fibres. The reactive dyes form a chemical bonding between the dye molecule and the fibre and because of the high temperature dyeing procedures involved they render excellent fastness properties to the dyed textiles.

(g) **Disperse Dyes:** Disperse dyes are usually used to dye re-generated manmade and few synthetic fibres like cellulose diacetate, cellulose triacetate, polyester and in certain combinations. Acrylic and nylon fibres are also dyed with disperse dyes. Satisfactory dyeing results are obtained with disperse dyes.

(h) **Sulphur Dyes:** Sulphur dyes are water insoluble dyes used for natural and manmade cellulosic fibres. Similar to the constitution of vat dyes, these are solublized or reduced by reagents like sodium sulphide or sodium hydrosulphite. Once the dye reaches the polymer system of the fibre, the reduced sulphur dye is converted to its original insoluble form by oxidation with an oxidizing agent like sodium perborate and gives satisfactory dyeing results when accompanied with high temperatures.

SELECTION OF DYES

Lasting beauty of colour is an important factor in consumers' finished goods. Durability of colour depends on (1) selection of the proper dye for the fiber to be dyed, (2) selection of the method of dyeing the fiber, yarn, or fabric.

The selection of dye for textiles depends upon the following factors:

- The type of dye used: Dyes have an affinity for the vegetable, animal or manmade fibres according the chemical constitution of the dye. Thus, the fibres having different chemical structures require different dyes.

- The degrees of fastness required to various conditions: i.e. fastness to washing, fastness to light and rubbing. Different dyes of different colours and chemical constitution have different degrees of fastness to various conditions. For example, a colour that may have good fastness to laundering may have poor fastness to light. Colour fastness may be affected by factors such as perspiration, dry cleaning, bleach, salt water, swimming pool additives, atmospheric gases, or air pollutants. Also, certain dyes may bleed, or run, when wet and many cause discolouration of other fabrics. Some dyes may crock, or rub off, due to the friction of wear.
- The ultimate use of the dyed textile: The selection of the proper dye is crucial to its ultimate use. Fastness to light is important in draperies, for example, as they must stand strong light daily but do not need to be washed frequently whereas fastness to washing is important in dress fabrics and household linen because they must undergo frequent washing. Therefore, both the kind of fibre to be dyed and the intended use for the fabric should be considered.

We shall now discuss some of the important methods for dyeing of textiles. There are different stages at which textiles could be dyed adopting different methods for the corresponding dyeing level, in dyeing houses and mills. **(Refer Plate 3.9)**

For fibre stage dyeing : **Stock dyeing method/Top dyeing method.**

For yarn stage dyeing : **(i) Hank dyeing**
(ii) Package dyeing
(iii) Warp beam dyeing
(iv) Space dyeing

For fabric stage: Piece dyeing method – **Union dyeing method**
– **Cross dyeing method**

In addition to these dyeing techniques for various dyeing stages, dyeing can also be carried out at the very initial polymer stage through **dope dyeing method** and also at the final stage through **garment dyeing method.**

STOCK DYEING METHOD

Stock dyeing method is used to dye staple fibres before they are spun. This method is usually used in case of natural fibres like wool or cotton. It consists of transferring the stock of fibres from the bale into dye baths and circulating dye liquor through the substrate at high temperatures (Refer Fig. 8.1).

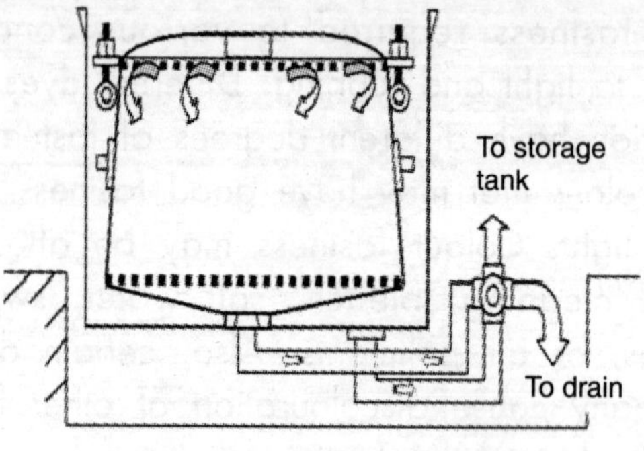

Fig 8.1 Stock syeing machine

TOP DYEING METHOD

One-step nearer to the finished yarn than stock dyeing is what is called top dyeing in the worsted industry. Top refers to wool that has been combed to take out the short fibres, and then delivered from the combs in a rope like form about 3cm thick. The top is wound on perforated spools and the dye liquor is *circulated* through the perforations of the spool. Very even dyeing is possible with this method.

YARN DYEING METHODS

Yarn dyeing is carried out at the stage after the fibre has been spun into the yarn. In this method the dyes penetrate into the fibres present along the length of the yarn and the fabrics made from these dyed yarns are termed as yarn-dyed fabrics. Yarn-dyed fabrics are usually deeper and richer in colour. The primary reason for dyeing in the yarn form is to create interesting checks, stripes, and plaids with different-coloured yarns; in the weaving process (for example, checked gingham, shepherd's check, plaid, seersucker etc.). Yarn dyeing can be carried out by different methods.

(i) **Hank Dyeing:** Yarn may be prepared in hank form and then dyed. The hanks are hung over a stand and immersed in a dye bath in a large container. The loose arrangement of the yarn allows for excellent dye penetration but is most costly method of yarn dyeing. Hank-dyed yarn is used to a considerable extent for suiting and dress goods.

(ii) **Package Dyeing:** Yarn wound on spools, cones or similar units in a packed form and then dyed is referred to as package dyed yarn. The packages of yarn are stacked on perforated rods in a rack and then immersed in a tank wherein the dye is forced outward from the rods under pressure through the spools and then back through the packages toward the center to penetrate the entire yarn as thoroughly as possible. Most carded and combed cotton that is used for knitted outerwear is package-dyed (Refer Fig. 8.2).

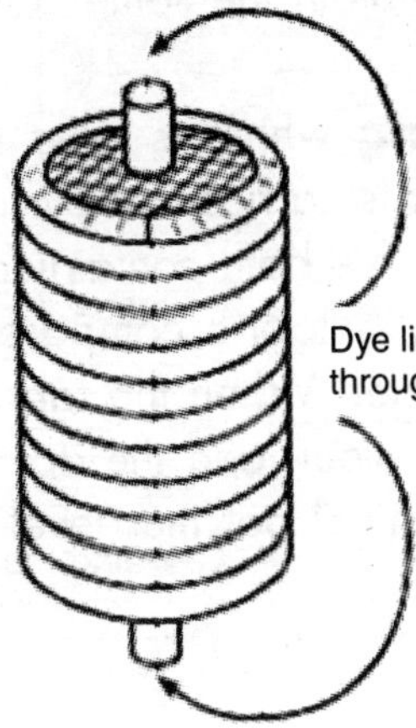

Fig 3.6 Package dyeing machine

(iii) **Warp-beam Dyeing:** In this method the yarn is wound onto a perforated warp beam, immersed in a tank, and dyed under pressure. This method is similar to package dyeing but is more economical. It is used when fabrics are to be woven with dyed warp yarns.

(iv) **Space Dyeing:** In this method the yarn is dyed at equal spaces and intervals along its length. One procedure is the knit-deknit method in which the yarn is knitted and the knitted cloth is then dyed, and it is subsequently deknitted. The dye penetrated the loops of the yarn but since it does not readily penetrate the areas of the yarn where it crosses itself, alternating dyed and undyed spaces appear, thus producing an ikat kind effect in the fabric.

PIECE DYEING METHOD

This method is adopted at fabric stage dyeing and is capable of bulk dyeing of fabric. Piece dyeing method gives satisfactory results with regard to levelness, penetration, and overall fastness.

Fabric may be piece dyed whether it is composed of one kind of fibre or yarn or of blends of different fibres or combinations of different yarns. When the fabric is made of one kind of fibre or yarn, then dyeing is relatively uncomplicated because only one appropriate dye is used. However, when the fabric contains a blend of fibres or combinations of different yarns, then special procedures are required which employ different dyes that are specific for the particular fibres used. These procedures are called union dyeing and cross-dyeing.

Union dyeing processes of dyeing fabrics made of different fibers or yarns is used in case if the dyeing is to be carried out in one single solid shade. Although different fibers may require different dyes to obtain the same colour, this may be done by putting the appropriate colour of dye.

Another method of **cross-dyeing** which is used to obtain two different coloured warps and wefts in a single fabric. It is carried out by immersing the fabric composed of two different types of fibers into one dye bath containing two different dyes, one specific for each of the fibers. For example, a fabric composed of viscose rayon and acetate yarns may be cross-dyed in this manner. When the fabric is removed from the dye bath, the viscose rayon yarns will be one colour, and the acetate yarns will be another colour.

The other methods of dyeing at initial polymer level and advanced apparel stage of dyeing are:

DOPE DYEING

Dope dyeing is carried out at the polymer level during the production of manmade fibres. A great deal of time and money can be saved and greater degree of colour fastness can be achieved, if the dye is added to the polymer solution or the Dope passing through the spinnerets into filaments.

GARMENT DYEING

Certain kinds of non-tailored apparel such as hosiery and sweaters can be dyed as completed garments because they are each made of a single component and will not be readily distorted.

A number of garments are loosely packed into a large nylon net bag. The bags are then put into a paddle dyer, which is a tub with a motor driven paddle that agitates the dye bath. Garment dyeing is an economical method.

Some other methods used for dyeing are termed as **jig/beck dyeing, pad dyeing, beam dyeing** and **jet dyeing**. These are different methods of dyeing textiles at various stages. These dyeing methods have their nomenclature based on the type of dyeing machineries used to dye the respective textile substrates.

CHAPTER 9

METHODS OF TEXTILE PRINTING

It is the accepted fact in the world of textiles that dyeing and printing processes provide lasting beauty and delight to the beholder by adding colour and design to fabrics. Dyeing and printing differ in the method by which colour is applied to fabric. In the dyeing processes, fiber, yarn, or fabric is impregnated with a dyestuff, in printing a pattern or a design is generally imprinted on the fabric in one or more colours by using dyes in form of paste or pigments. Printing of fabric by various traditional methods occupies a unique place in the history of civilization. It has been handed down from generation to generation. Block printing is perhaps the oldest and most commonly used technique of surface ornamentation.

India has been famous for its textiles from very early times as revealed by literary and archaeological evidence. The origin of printing as hard to trace, but it is known that, it existed in the pre Christian era and records show that printed goods from India were going west more then a 1000 years ago (Refer Fig. 9.1).

Fig 9.1 The earliest Egyptian printed cloth with soft clay blocks from Egypt - 4th century

Fragment of a madder dyed fabric discovered at Mohenjodaros excavation and patterned cloth on the sculpture of that time gives the evidence of cotton spinning, weaving and patterning in India as early as 3000 BC. Also, resist dyed textile pieces and the blocks made of soft clay have been found in the tombs of Egypt dated around the 4th century. Some authorities claim that the printed clothing seen in Ajanta Frescoes is illustrative of block printing. Also, said is, that China was the inventor of block printing, the country which produced the first printed books.

Thus, one form of applying colour decoration to a fabric after it has otherwise been finished is called printing. Fabric that is to be printed must be singed, bleached and cleaned. From plain dyeing printing is a means of producing more colourful effects on textiles. There are three basic approaches to printing a colour on a fabric; direct, discharge, and resist.

DIRECT PRINTING

The technique of direct printing is most commonly used for applying coloured pattern to the fabric. It may be done on a white fabric or over a previously dyed fabric. The dye is imprinted on the fabric in paste form and any desired pattern may be produced. The dyes or the pigments used are usually dissolved in a limited amount of water to which is thickening and binding agents like corn starch, resins, gums, alginates are added to give necessary viscosity to the print paste and allows better penetration of colour, which is important for good printing process. These pigments have excellent fastness to washing and according to the choice of pigment this can be supplemented by excellent fastness to light, perspiration and other harmful influences.

Direct printing is carried out by any of the usual methods, such as block, stencil, roller or screen printing.

DISCHARGE PRINTING

Another approach for applying a colour pattern is discharge printing, which produces attractive prints usually in white on a coloured background **(Refer Plate 3.10)**. In this process the fabric is dyed through piece dyeing method in dark colour and then printed with a chemical to destroy the colour in desired areas. Sometimes the base colour is removed and another colour printed in its place, thus discharging or extracting the colour hence the name discharge printing.

To produce a white polka dot pattern on a ground colour, the fabric is first dyed with a ground shade; say blue then it is printed with a paste containing chemicals capable of bleaching the blue colour to a white. Such a paste is called a discharge paste. Discharge prints are found on cottons and rayons and in some patterned silks with dark backgrounds. Special care is required on part of the consumers if he desires serviceability form discharge printed fabric, since the chemical that discharges the dye tends to weaken the fabric in the area of the design.

RESIST PRINTING

This technique of printing is one of the oldest technique. The print pattern is achieved when the bleached goods are printed with a resin or a resist paste through which the dye or pigment paste cannot penetrate. After the fabric has passed thorough subsequent dyeing process, the resist paste is removed leaving a pattern on a dark ground. The dye is fixed everywhere except where the resist pattern has been printed. Thus the result obtained is a white pattern on a coloured ground similar to the discharge technique of printing. In the discharge method the fabric is first dyed and the colour is then extracted by a reducing agent; in the resist method, a resist paste is first imprinted and the fabric is then dyed. The durability of the fabric is not affected by the resist method.

Some manual printing methods, applied using these printing approaches are as follows:

Block Printing

The oldest and most popular method of directly printing patterns on fabric is block printing by hand. It is relatively slow method of printing but is extensively used to print lengths of materials for dress and linens. In India Rajasthan, Gujarat and Uttar Pradesh are the chief centers of block printing. To make blocked prints, the design must first be carved on a wooden metal or lilonium blocks **(Refer Plate 3.11)**. It consists of carving a thick block of wood so that a pattern stands out in relief. This block is dipped in a colour paste and then pressed down firmly by hand on selected portions upon the fabric so that the coloured pattern is transferred to it **(Refer Plate 3.12)**.

Hand blocked prints can be recognized by slight irregularities in the details and in the repetition of the design. Block printing usually gives bold patterns but can be made to very fine patterns where exclusive patterns are required. **(Refer Plate 3.13)** But for mass producing printed fabrics the method used is roller printing. This method of producing attractive designs is relatively inexpensive when compared with any hand method. It is a machine counterpart of block printing. In roller printing engraved copper cylinders or rollers take the place of the hand carved blocks but it lacks to render exclusivity in designs, patterns and colour combinations.

Stencil Printing

Stencil printing is the simplest method of printing originated in Japan. In stencil printing, the design must first be cut on cardboard, wood, or metal. The stencil may have a fine, delicate design, or bold patterns through which a great amount of colour can be applied. The stencil printing process can be accomplished with the help of a cotton swabs, brushes or air pressure pumps, each giving the desired effects. A stencil design is usually limited to the application of 2-3 colours and is generally used for printing fewer repeats on a narrow width of fabric.

Screen Printing

Screen printing is another manual method of direct printing, originally referred to as silk-screen printing because the screens were made of fine, strong silk threads. Today, they are also made of nylon, polyester, vinyl, and metal. Screen printing is done with the use of either flat or cylindrical screens. Screen printing is adapted from the technique of stencil printing. The ordinary stencils designs are transferred on a screen mesh fastened on to a wooden frame. Then the screen is coated with an enamel paint or varnish of hardened gelatine leaving the design portion open, according to the design or pattern. More usually, today, the design is photographed and a negative is used for each sensitized screen to opaque, or block out, those areas not part of the screen's colour design. A separate screen is required for each colour. The printing paste, or dye, is poured on the screen and forced through the unblocked areas onto the fabric with rubber-edged squeeze. The frame is then raised and placed on the next section of the fabric, and the operation is repeated until the entire length of the cloth is printed with that one colour. According to the number of colours the design has, each step is repeated until the fabric is completely covered with the pattern **(Refer Plate 3.14)**.

The result obtained by screen printing are more attractive and pleasing as up to fourteen or even sixteen colours in one pattern can be produced. Thus screen printing has these days become a very useful printing method since it offers scope of devising new and creative ideas and one can work with wide range of colours, for textiles, furnishings, leaflets, banners etc. **(Refer Plate 3.15)**

Flat screen printing is usually done by hand, but now the process is mechanized. This process is called rotary screen printing in which the screen and the squeeze moves on a conveyor belt. The machine employs a rotary screen for each colour, as in flat screen printing producing prints of various types and intricate designs with shades of up to twenty colours. Their production output is considerable higher than of flat screen machines.

Batik Dyeing

The resist-dyeing process, whereby designs are made with wax on a fabric which is subsequently immersed in a dye to absorb the colour on the unwaxed portions, is known as batik dyeing. This art was first originated on the island of Java; in Indonesia and then routed to eastern India, and was revived in Shantinikaten (Kolkata of Bengal) in India and has now spread in various parts of India and to some extent in Japan, Europe and parts of Africa.

The patterns for batik are artistic designs drawn by hand. The patterns are generally in geometrical, floral, bird or animal motifs, and other stylized forms **(Refer Plate 3.16)**. The motif is drawn on cotton cambric. Then melted wax mixed with a resin is traced on the areas not to be dyed or through which the passage of the dye paste is to be restricted. The application of the wax must be done on both sides of fabric. After each application of wax, the fabric is dipped into dye to obtain the particular colour desired. Only that portion of the fabric that is not covered by the wax will absorb the dye, as the wax coating on the rest of the cloth serves as a resist. After the dye has been fixed and the material dried, the cloth is boiled and rinsed to remove the wax. Any traces of wax remaining on the fabric are then scraped off. This procedure is repeated depending upon the number of colours present in the design composition. The commonly used colours for batik are usually combinations of bright and dull colours namely red, yellow, and blue, and dark shades of brown, green, violet, orange, and pink are also used.

Though, this method of making the print is a slow process, it gives exclusive results similar to hand painting. **(Refer Plate 3.17)**

Tie Dyeing

As the name suggests the fabric is first tied and then dyed. The dye is resisted by knots that are tied in the cloth before it is immersed in the dye bath. The outside of the knotted portion is dyed, but the inside is not penetrated if the knot is firmly tied. Different knotting techniques and by inserting different materials like pencils, screws, threads, coins give varied print effects. Like other hand methods, tie dyeing is expensive. Because this methods creates interesting design and patterns dyed with direct dyes yielding dark and bright colours, hence is more popular printing technique with the masses **(Refer Plate 3.18)**.

Ikat Dyeing

Ikat dyeing is the process similar to tie and dye with the basic difference being that in former case the fabric is the base material while in the later case the yarns are tied and dyed. This is an ancient method of fabric colouration by tie-dyeing bundles of warp and/or weft yarns prior to weaving. It is believed to have originated in Japan then migrated and Bali, Java, and Sumatra. In India this art originated from Gujarat, Andhra Pradesh, Orissa and other eastern states.

Ikat is skilled art form. The colours, usually shades of orange, green, indigo, red, and brown, are placed along the length of the yarns in anticipation of the design that is the woven. When the fabric is woven, the edges of the design have a blurred or shimmering effect thus creating a pattern that has its own charm and uniqueness. This is probable the most expensive of all manual printing techniques due to extensive labour and great precision involved in rendering this technique.

One most important point that is to be kept in mind after completion of all the printing techniques is their after-treatment and fixation of the prints on to the surface of the fabric by heat setting or curing them in an oven at specific temperatures depending on the base fabric and dyes/pigments used.

In recent years due to the technological advancements and in order to cater to need and demands of the consumer several newer printing techniques have emerged. Like **roller printing, transfer printing, blotch printing, electrostatic printing, photo printing; digital-analog printing** to name a few. All these techniques are much faster, efficient and precise as compared to manual methods of printing but as they are mass produced they lack in their uniqueness in terms of patterns, design composition, colours and other related aspects **(Refer Plate 3.19, 3.20)**.

TEXTILE DESIGN PROCESS

Section IV

Learning objectives:

By the end of this section, the following aspects of textile design would be clear:

- What is a good design.
- The elements of art: line, shape, form, texture, colour.
- The fundamental art principles of design viz., balance, properties, rhythm, emphasis.
- Colour as one of the most important art element in the design.
- The basic colour schemes and their application as per the effects required
- Creating textile designs and repeat patterns.

CHAPTER 10

ELEMENTS AND PRINCIPLES OF DESIGN

ELEMENTS OF DESIGN

A design is a deliberate or well considered plan, not a hit-or-miss result. Design is defined as an arrangement of lines, forms, space, textures and colours. It involves the problem of choosing these elements and arranging them in order to get a good result. Beauty in design can be achieved through order and functional restraint. To create or judge in good taste, it is helpful to rely on fundamental art principles of design which are the building blocks of any design composition.

The elements of design are the basic components used as part of any design. They are the objects to be arranged, the constituent parts used to create the composition itself. In most situations the elements of design build upon one another, the former element helping to create the latter. We will be focusing on the main elements of line, form (shape), texture and colour.

LINE

Line is an important element of art and a base of a good design. Line provides a path of vision along which the eye may travel from one point to another. It defines the position and direction of the design.

A line is an element characterized by length and direction. Lines create contours and form, and are often used to convey a specific kind of feeling or point to an important feature in a design. The line may be straight and direct or it may turn in different ways. Even when the line is broken, the eye tends to connect points in space to form a linear pattern. In addition, lines that are grouped together often create a sense of value, density or texture.

A line can vary in length, width, direction, curvature, and colour. Line can be two-dimensional (a pencil line on paper), or implied three-dimensional.

Lines can be straight, curved or irregularly shaped as illustrated in Fig. 10.1

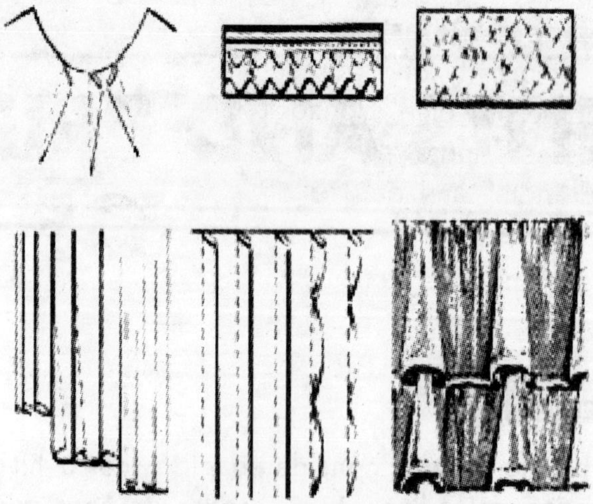

Fig. 10.1 Use of lines in clothing

The expressiveness of line is determined by its function, type, direction and quality. There are two types of lines – structural and decorative, denoted as in case of garments/ apparels.

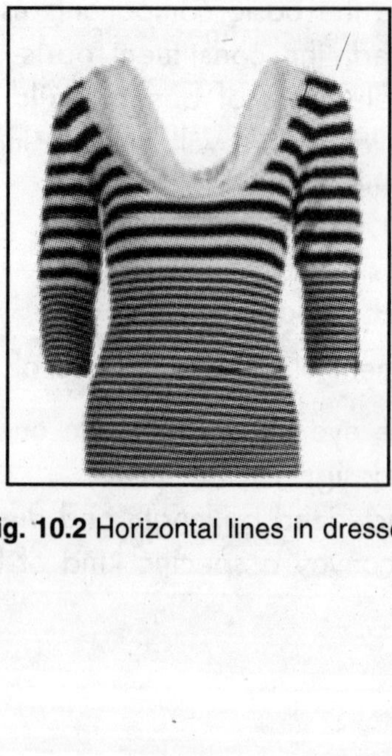

Fig. 10.2 Horizontal lines in dresses

Structural Lines: Are the actual lines that result from the making of a garment, such as seams, hemlines, edges and folds.

Decorative Lines: Are the applied, or superimposed, lines that result from the placement of trim and ornamentation on the apparels.

A line defines the outline of a design and divides it in to various parts. **Line direction** has a definite effect on your apparent proportion. The expression of these lines are expressed by the position of the body.

Horizontal Lines: (Refer Plate 4.1). When a person is resting or sleeping, it suggests the pull of gravity and parallel objects in rest and repose. (i.e., surface of earth, a quiet expanse of water). Horizontal lines influence rest and relaxation. Horizontal lines suggest reposeness, passiveness, steadiness, duration. These lines usually have the effect of width, breadth, and generally heavy built. People are advised not to wear these lines (Refer Fig 10.2).

Vertical Lines: The most common use of line is to control the flow, direction and speed of the viewer's eye. Vertical lines will stop the person's eye, and give a sensation of mass and volume. They can also convey power and strength. It carries the eye in the upward rising movement and is usually associated with dignity and formally (example: tall buildings, a king's poise) **(Refer Plate 4.2)**.

These lines manifest the feeling of poise, strength, stability, uprightness, aspiration. They also impose grandeur, stateliness or an impression of added height. The reason for which obese people and short heighted individuals are advised to wear textiles/apparels constituting vertical lines (Refer Fig. 10.3).

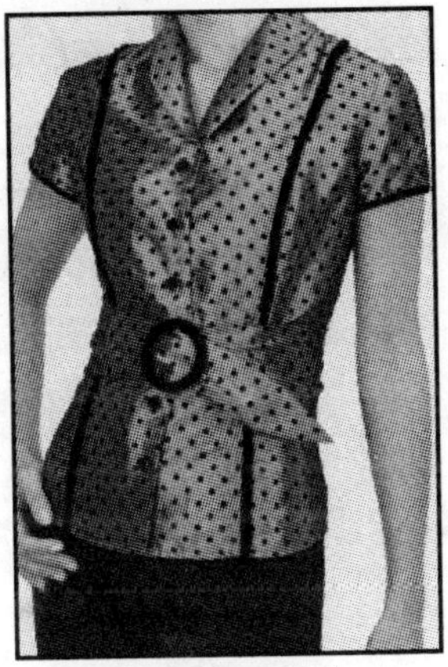

Fig. 10.3 Vertical lines in a dress

Curved Lines: They may vary from gentle undulation to full rounded convolution. The gradual transition in the change of direction imparts a slow but rhythmic quality to the line **(Refer Plate 4.3)**. When a person is in action, the body takes curves, so curved lines are gracious and flexible, flowing and gentle. Lines that are vigorously curved tend to be more active in character (Refer Fig. 10.4).

Fig. 10.4 Curved lines features in a dress

Diagonal Lines: Diagonal lines are dynamic and active. These suggest movement, force and express sophistication and refinement **(Refer Plate 4.4)**. When we run or are otherwise unusually active, our bodies assume a diagonal position, head thrust forward. A diagonal line is longer than a perpendicular line and may sometimes used to convey height and at times width (Refer Fig. 10.5).

Fig.. 10.5 Diagonal lines in clothing

Lines may be gay and humorous, stiff and severe, light and delicate or awkwardly heavy. It all depends on the size and thickness of line, its placement with total composition and the degree of contrast it enjoys with other elements. Any of the given lines can dominate in a good design or composition to symbolise their respective qualities (Refer Fig. 10.6), which are as follows:

1. *Horizontal:* The line of growth, loftiness and inspiration.
2. *Vertical:* The lines of tranquality and repose.
3. *Diagonal:* The line of motion, progression and unrest.
4. *Oblique:* (Alternating) The dynamic lines suggest speed or flight.
5. *Converging:* Line pointing upwards are dynamic, may also suggest loftiness.
6. *Semi Circle:* (The arc) It is joyous and graceful, the line found in nature.
7. *Wavy Lines:* This is the lyric line of beauty, suggesting liquid, continuity or following motion.

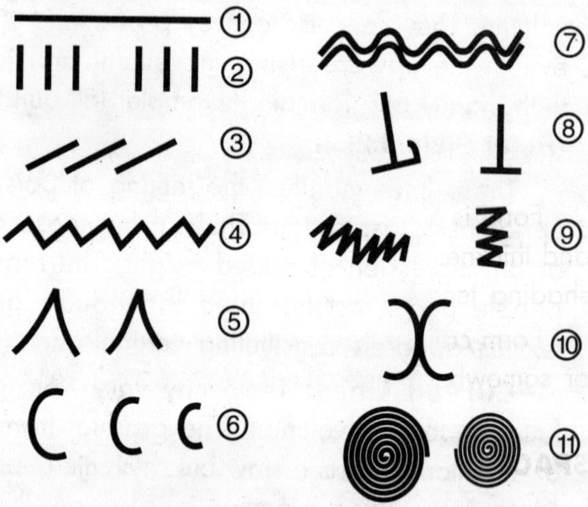

Fig. 10.6 Types of lines

8. *Opposing:* (Straight) are lines that attract attention, may be disturbing unless used creatively or constructively.
9. *Zig-Zag:* The lightening lines suggest chaos or conflict.
10. *Opposing Curves:* Branching lines of nature, they suggest growth, progression and harmony of movement.
11. *Spiral Line:* The continuous line, one of nature's shell designs. It suggests depth.

SHAPE/FORM

The next element of design is shape which is a closed line. Shape is distinguished from its surroundings by its outline within the design. Shape is a 2-dimensional line with no form or thickness and can express length and width.

A flat figure, shape is created when actual or implied lines meet to surround a space. A change in colour or shading can define a shape. The simplest definition of shape is a closed contour, an element defined by its perimeter. Shapes can be divided into several types: geometric (square, triangle, circle) and organic (irregular in outline).

Any 2 - dimensional object is called a shape, and **Forms** are three - dimensional shapes, expressing length, width, and depth. Balls, cylinders, boxes and triangles are forms.

Shape 2-D **Form 3-D**

Form is similar to the idea of shape. Form is the structure of the design having volume and thickness. It is the illusion of a 3-D effect that can be implied with the use of light and shading techniques. Form can be viewed from many angles.

Form can be both two-dimensional and three-dimensional and can be realistic, abstract or somewhere in between. The terms form and shape are often used synonymously.

SPACE

Space is the empty or open area between and around objects. Space has to be included in the design which means leaving some blank areas in and around the design.

The space around objects is often called negative space; negative space has shape. Negative space gives direction by leading the eye into positive space. The balance between the use of negative space and positive space will make an image look "right". Positive space is filled by a shape or form. Negative space surrounds a shape or form **(Refer Plate 4.5)**.

Space can also be suggested by the use of tone, colour and the linear perspective of overlapping planes.

TEXTURE

The word has its origin from the Latin "Textura" meaning weaving. The word is invariably used to mean the surface appearance or quality (visual property) and the feel (tactile property) of the substance (fabric) for practical and decorative purposes.

Visual texture is one which is apparent to the eye, for example gloss of a glass tile, stiffness of an organdy fabric, where as tactile texture can be appreciated by touching them, for example roughness of the bark of a tree, smoothness of a satin fabric.

The hand and character of the fabric depends upon the fibre, yarn and weave used and the finished applied or any super imposed pattern example printing, embroidery etc.

Textures can be	Smooth	-	Rough
	Fine	-	Coarse
	Supple	-	Stiff
	Lustrous	-	Dull
	Metallic	-	Stony
	Transparent	-	Opaque

Texture affects, colour, drape and silhouette. Different fabrics absorb dye (colour) differently and, according to closeness or looseness of their weave absorb and reflect light differently. Smooth textures reflect light, making more intense the colour while rough textures absorb light, making a colour appear duller.

Example: The black colour of a silk will appear more brighter as compared to black colour of a woolen fabric which would appear to be darker and duller **(Refer Plate 4.6)**.

A texture could be light (organdy) medium (linen) and heavy (worsted). The weight of the material would partially determine its behaviour and function. i.e. some fabrics will drape well, while others can be tailored and moulded to your figure. Example: clinging fabrics like chiffon will reveal the contours of the body. Therefore, it is suitable for well defined feminine figure. Heavy textures would add bulk, thus making it unsuitable for short and stout figures.

Also, soft textures would serve best for style with gathers, while stiff or crisp textures stand away from the body, increasing the apparent size and can be well used to hide figure defects **(Refer Plate 4.7)**.

Texture as an element of art can be intelligently and interestingly used to create contrast which appeals more. At the same time it is more important that one texture dominates. Thus, texture helps your design to be distinctive or have identifying character and characteristics. With the proper texture, your design will look more fascinating than the average design.

COLOUR

Colour is more important than line or texture in giving interest to a design. It tends to attract and hold attention to a greater extent than any other art element. Colour is obtained due to refraction of light through a prism. When white light falls on the prism it refracts and a spectrum is obtained in the form seven colours (VIBGYOR) **(Refer Plate 4.8)**. Based on this physical phenomenon, there are many different kinds of colour systems, and many different theories on colour. For now we will focus on the basics, using a colour wheel for illustration purposes. There are three main components of colour or colour has three dimensions – hue, value and saturation.

Hue: It is the name by which we distinguish, one colour from another or can be defined as to where the colour is positioned in the colour wheel. The three main hues are red, blue and yellow. These are called pure/basic/primary colours because all other colours are obtained from them.

Value: Value is the relative darkness or lightness of a colour. In general, how close to black or white a given colour is refers to the amount or degree of lightness or darkness of a colour. Light colours such as sky blue, pastel pink etc., are called tints and dark colours such as navy blue, maroon are called shades. Like texture, value can be used to bring objects closer, make them seem more distant — higher value contrast brings them closer(tints), and a duller contrast pushes them further away(shades).

Value can also be used to give focus to certain areas and to make others seem less important.

Saturation Intensity: It refers to the brightness or dullness of a colour such as bright red, i.e. scarlet used in full intensity. A bright colour can be subdued by mixing grey colour into it. The more grey a colour, the less intense or saturated it is. **(Refer Plate 4.9)**

Apart from these dimensions, colours possess properties of temperature and force.

Property of Temperature: This indicates warm and cool colours.

Warm colours are those which convey warmth yellow, yellow orange, red, red orange, orange, while cool colours are those which convey feeling of coolness. They are violet, blue, green **(Refer Plate 4.10)**.

Property of Force: It indicates advancing and receding colours.

Advancing colours are those which make an object appear larger and closer. They are bright colours which attracts attention easily. Receding colours are subdued and lighter tones of all colours. They make an object appear distant.

These properties are better understood, through colour wheel.

The colour wheel is a way of showing the chromatic scale in a circle using all the colours made with the primary triad. The colour wheel consists of six basic colours. It consists of three primary colours (red, blue, yellow), three secondary colours (violet, green, orange) and six intermediate colours (red orange, red violet, blue violet, blue green, yellow green, yellow orange).

When two primary colours are mixed a secondary colour is obtained example yellow + red = orange. Intermediate colours or tertiary colours are obtained when one primary colour and one secondary colour are mixed. Example: yellow + orange = yellow orange. **(Refer Plate 4.11)**

Colour also has certain adjectives, with each colour denoting certain psychological qualities. For example,

- Black: The colour of authority and power.
- White: Denotes Innocence and purity.
- Red: Red is the most stimulating colour on the colour wheel. It can stimulate faster heart rate, influence anger, and appetite.
- Blue: Blue invokes peace, tranquility and loyalty, but can also be cold and depressing.
- Green: A difficult colour to master, yet it is one of the most relaxing. Dark green is masculine and conservative, and implies wealth.
- Purple: Is the colour of royalty, and gives the impression of luxury, wealth and sophistication.

Thus, colour being one of the major art element, has different colour harmonies, combinations and various other concepts which would be discussed in the coming chapter.

These elements of design are used to create the principles of design. Principles are the results of using the elements. The principles of design are the recipe for a good work of art. The principles combine the elements to create an aesthetic placement of things that will produce a good design.

There are many basic concepts that underly the principles of design. Few of the important principles of design can be classified as;

1. Balance 2. Proportion 3. Rhythm 4. Emphasis 5. Harmony

BALANCE

Balance is as fundamental in visual arts as it is in life itself. It produces a feeling of rest. It is the result of the equalization of attractions on either side of a central point. Balance must be attained in colour, texture, pattern, light as well as in weight.

For example, a balanced pattern has a border on the pattern in black. Unbalanced would be if approximately one-third of the border was orange and the other two-thirds in pink. To keep design balanced, the measurements should be as accurate as possible. Keeping the design symmetric is a good technique for good balance, but not necessarily the best for all types of designs. There are three types of balance: **1. Formal or Symmetrical, 2. Informal or Asymmetrical, 3. Radial Balance** (Refer Plate **4.12**).

Formal Balance results when objects of equal weight are placed on each side and at the equal distances form the center, when they are identical the balance is formal or symmetrical. Under normal circumstances it assumes identical forms on both sides of the axis. In addition, it is possible to build a composition equally around a central point resulting in radial balance symmetry.

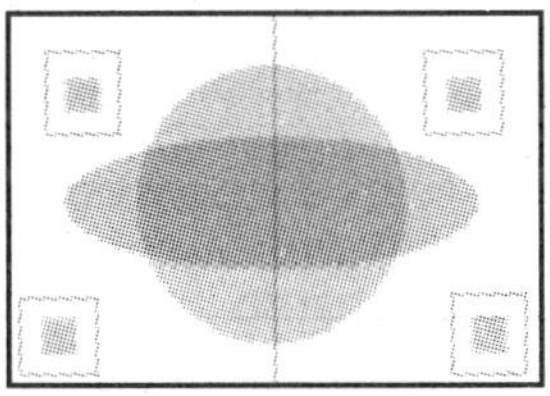

Formal balance or symmetry

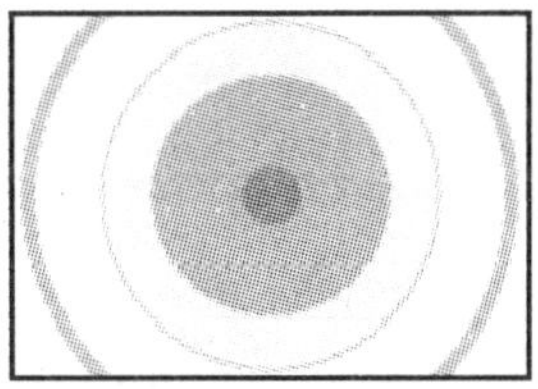

Radial symmetry

Formal balance gives a feelings of neatness, strength, straight forwardness, thus it seems suitable for tailored clothes which have same pockets, tucks or darts on one side as on the other (Refer Fig 10.7).

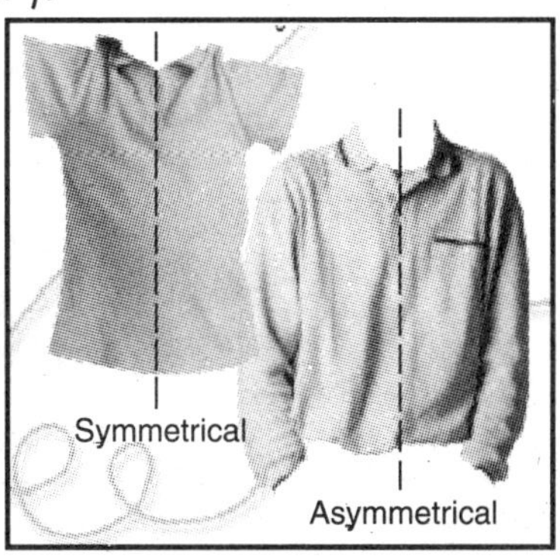

Fig. 10.7 Balance created in a garment

Informal Balance also called the asymmetrical balance results when objects are so arranged that large one near the center balances a small one from the center. Asymmetrical balance occurs when the weight of a composition is not evenly distributed around a central axis.

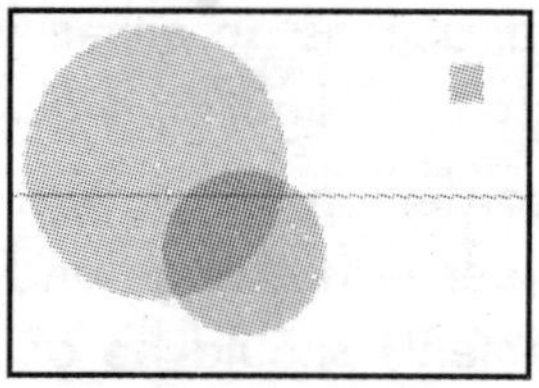

Informal balance or asymmetry

It is more creative than formal balance, because there are no rules or regulations to guide one in its production.

Informal balance is not easy to achieve or analyse. It is softer, more graceful due to transitional lines, and suited to gay or dramatic moods dresses. Radial balance is equidistant balance created around the radius of the design composition.

Thus, a balance in a composition can be created through different elements of design. **(Refer Plate 4.13)**

PROPORTION

It gives pleasing space divisions. It states the relation between parts of design with each other and with the whole. It deals with relationship in size, shape, colour, light, texture and pattern. Differing proportions within a composition can relate to different kinds of balance or symmetry, and can establish visual weight and depth **(Refer Plate 4.14)**. For a design to be pleasing, the parts should be close enough in size to appear to belong together but varied enough to apply interest. The human figure is considered to be of beautiful proportion. If it were to be divided into eight equal parts then three parts fall above the hollow of waist and five below it.

In the below examples, notice how the smaller elements seem to receed into the background while the larger elements come to the front.

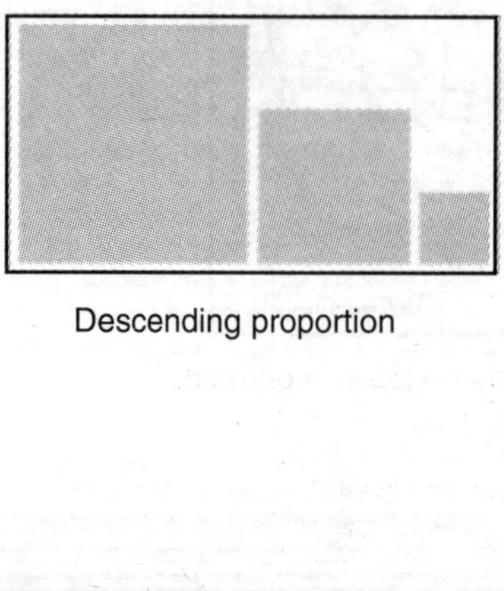

Descending proportion

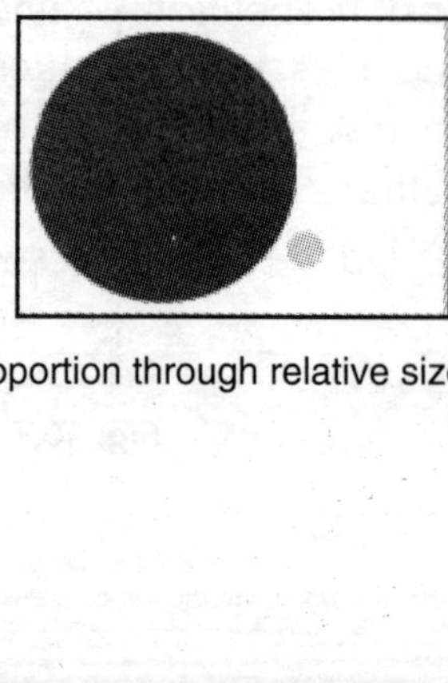

Proportion through relative sizes

RHYTHM

It is that quality of deign which imparts, graceful, flowing movement through out the design. The process of leading the eye from one part to the other in a design is termed as rhythm **(Refer Plate 4.15)**.

What rhythm in music is to the ear, the same is rhythm in design is to the eye. Rhythm is a feeling of organized movement which is smooth, and has variety which is essential to keep rhythm exciting and active, and moving the viewer around the artwork **(Refer Plate 4.16)**.

For example a plain white box has almost no rhythm what so ever.

Thus, variety in rhythm can create a sense of movement, and can establish pattern and texture. There are many different kinds of rhythm, often defined by the feeling it evokes when looking at it.

Regular: A regular rhythm occurs when the intervals between the elements, and often the elements themselves, are similar in size or length.

Flowing: A flowing rhythm gives a sense of movement, and is often more organic in nature.

Progressive: A progressive rhythm shows a sequence of forms through a progression of steps.

Regular rhythm

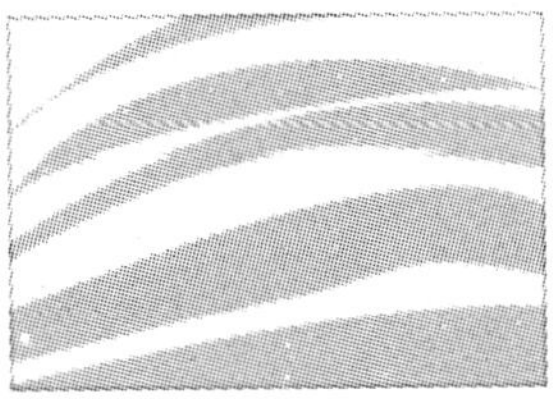

Flowing rhythm

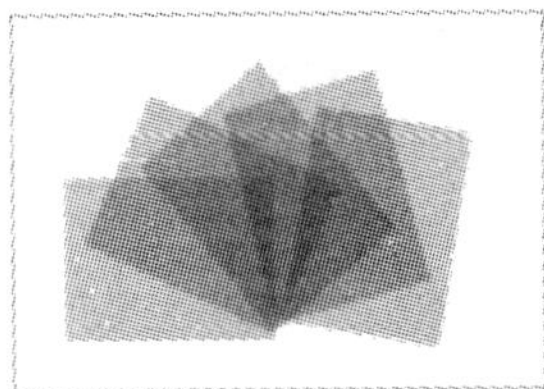

Progressive rhythm

These different kinds of rhythm can be produced by:

- Repetition • Transition
- Gradation – Progression or regression
- Opposition • Radiation

Repetition: Repetition of lines, shapes, textures or colours can produce rhythmic pattern. It can also be achieved by repetition of buttons, ruffles, rows of machining in a garment (refer Fig. 10.8).

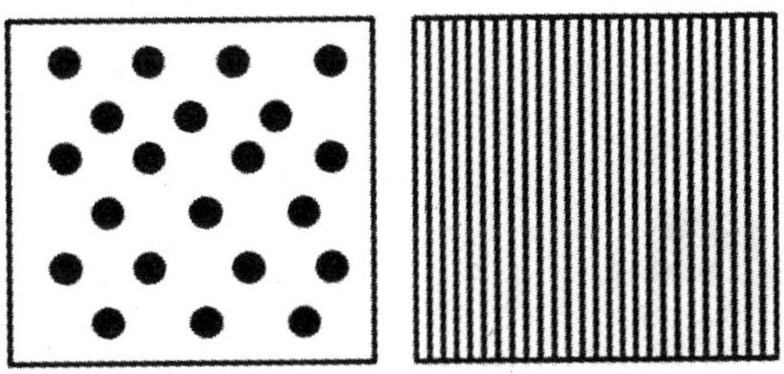

Fig. 10.8 Rhythm through repetition

Transition: Is secured when two lines gradually come together from different directions. Transitional lines and shapes which do not show value contrasts are preferred which are conspicuous and have zig-zag movement (refer Fig. 10.9).

Fig. 10.9 Rhythm through transition

Gradation: It is rhythm that suggests a gradual increase or decrease in shapes, sizes, colours, textures, lines etc., such as tucks of increase length or increase in the size of the print on a fabric. Colours may progress from bright to grey and textures from dull to shiny (refer Fig. 10.10).

Fig. 10.10 Rhythm through gradation

Opposition: When two or more lines run in opposite direction, they exemplify rhythm by opposition. Examples, Yokes, pleats and construction lines in the garments (Refer Fig. 10.11).

Fig. 10.11 Rhythm through opposition.

Radiation: It is the rhythm obtained by lines starting from a center point and flowing out into an arc such as that produced by bows, frills at the neckline (refer Fig. 10.12) in garments.

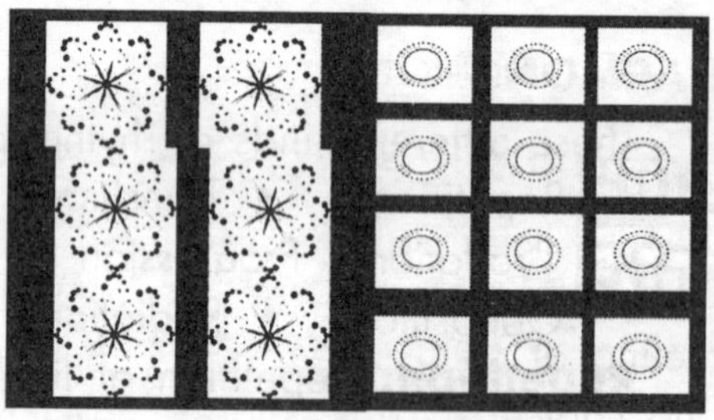

Fig. 10.12 Rhythm created through radiation in a design

EMPHASIS

It is dominance of part with subordination of others. It is that design principle by which the eye is led first to the most important part and then to the other parts in order of their importance **(Refer Plate 4.17)**. An object gains emphasis if given enough plain space for the background. This principle of design can be applied to one's clothes by accentuating one's good point and concealing one's defects. In applying such a principle it is necessary to know three things.

- What to emphasize.
- How to emphasize.
- How much to emphasize.

Simplicity is the keynote to all good designs, but when doubtful it is better to under emphasize rather than over emphasize a design.

Emphasis is given to an area within the design because that area is meant to be seen or is more important to be noticed when compared to other places of the design. For example, a design has white parallel lines going up and down. The center of this design, has a circle. This circle would be a part of the design that is emphasized.

Thus, Emphasis is the part of the design that catches the viewer's attention. Usually an artist makes one area stand out by contrasting it with other areas with respect to size, colour, texture, shape, etc. Likewise, emphasis is created here through a bright red coloured dot present.

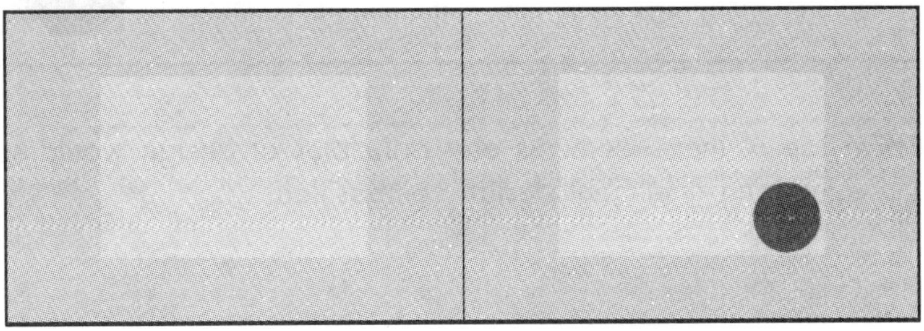

HARMONY

It is relatedness without sameness; suitability **(Refer Plate 4.18)**. It conveys a feeling of unity (oneness) without monotony throughout the design by appropriate use and choice of lines, shapes, forms, textures, size, value, intensity of colour, feeling, or ideas. When all the principles of art are followed it will result in complete harmony/unity of design. In order to secure harmony in a design, the following rules must be observed:

- Spaces must be interestingly distributed.
- Shapes must be similar and properly balanced.
- Structural and decorative lines must be consistent.

- Texture must be pleasingly combined.
- Ideas must be related.

If a design composition has wavy lines and organic shapes present, the use of geometric shapes in the same, would not result in harmony of the design.

This concept of unity describes the relationship between the individual parts and the whole of a composition. It investigates the aspects of a given design that are necessary to tie the composition together, to give it a sense of wholeness, or to break it apart and give it a sense of variety. An example of a graphic showing sameness and relatedness harmonized in a pattern.

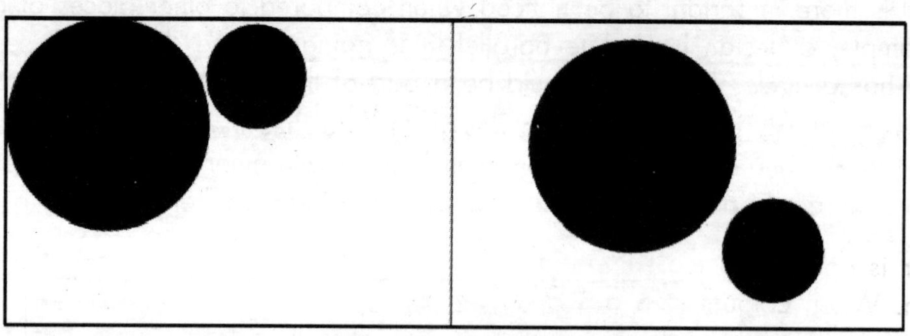

Thus, effective use of these elements and principles of design would surely lead to creation of a creative and intelligent design composition.

CHAPTER 11

COLOUR HARMONIES

Colour is one of the most important feature of art. Colours, renders a meaning to the design. When colours in a design are in harmony it is a pleasing sensation but when colours clash you experience discord. For example, a bright red colour design on a parrot green base illustrates discord, but when colours are too similar you experience monotony. Colour harmony can be

(a) Similar and related colour harmony.

(b) Contrasting colour harmony.

SIMILAR AND RELATED COLOUR HARMONY

They are those produced from colours that lie adjacent to each other on the colour wheel. The two related colour harmony are monochromatic colour harmony and analogous colour harmony.

- **Monochromatic Colour Harmony** means one colour harmony, where mono is one and chroma is colour. Several values of one colour illustrates this harmony. Example: sky blue – blue – navy blue. **(Refer Plate 4.19)**
- **Analogous Colour Harmony** is a combination of neighbouring colours with one colour in common. Example: yellow green, yellow, yellow orange, illustrate analogous colour harmony where yellow is common. Analogous colours tend to be families of colours such as blues (blue, blue-violet, blue-green) and yellows (yellow, yellow-orange, yellow-green) **(Refer Plate 4.20)**.

- **Contrasting Colour Harmony:** Contrasting colours are produced by combining colours that are far apart on the colour wheel. The contrasting colour harmonies are used in accordance with the Law of areas. Light, dark or dull colours should be used in largest areas. Neutral colours in the next largest area and bright colours or colours with full intensity should be applied in small areas.

The four contrasting harmony frequently used are:

(i) Complementary

(ii) Split Complementary

(iii) Triad

(iv) Accentuated Neutral

Complementary Harmony is obtained by using two colours exactly opposite to each other on the colour wheel. Example: blue and orange; red and green. When complementary colours are placed side-by-side they tend to enhance the intensity (chroma) of each other, and when they are blended together they tend to decrease the intensity of each other **(Refer Plate 4.21)**.

Spilt Complementary Harmony is obtained by choosing the colours, for instance red and the colours on either side of its complement i.e. yellow green and blue green (omitting the complementary) **(Refer Plate 4.22)**.

Traid Colour Harmony is a combination of any three colours that form an equilateral triangle on the colour wheel. This harmony combines the three primary colours or the three secondary colours or three intermediate colours **(Refer Plate 4.23)**.

Accentuated Neutral Colour Harmony is the one in which the largest areas are in neutral colours such as grey, white or black with one bright colour used to highlight the design. This is a very effective harmony. Example: if a costume of grey or black colour is worn the accessories are of red colour it illustrates an Accentuated Neutral Colour Harmony.

Thus, colour harmonies serve to describe the relationships certain colours have to one another, and how they can be combined to create a palette of colour.

Keeping in consideration the theme, the different moods of the colours, a textile designer should develop designs and prints best suited for its composition.

Factors that influence the choice of colours of textiles/apparels

When you spend money for a garment you want to look and feel your best in it. If colours are not in harmony with your personality and mood you will look uninteresting. Although personal colouring is of primary importance, other factors also influence the choice of colours.

(i) Season
(ii) Fashion
(iii) Occasion
(iv) Size and Personality
(v) Ward robe
(vi) Personal Colouring

Season: During winter season, black, brown, dark reds, dark green etc., are predominant providing warmth whereas in the spring time pastels, beige, blue, white, grey are the main colours worn due to their association with coolness.

Fashion: Each year colours are introduced in various new names dictated by fashion season and number of new colours become popular because they sound different from the preceding season. Therefore, the choice of colour is also influenced by the colour forecast by the designers.

Occasion: Colours are definitely associated with certain occasions. A lemon yellow, a sky blue, pastel pink will look lovely for a summer day time party dress. A bright red, a blue or black would look sensational for a dinner cum dance party at night. White is suitable for religious occasion.

Size and Personality: Colours can make a person look large or tiny. In others words it can increase or reduce one's size. You may look much lighter and slimmer in black. If white and tints of colours are worn by bony persons it will make their figures look fuller and healthier.

Wardrobe: Budgets influences the choice of colours in a wardrobe. With an unlimited budget it is possible to have different colours matching accessories with all outfits. It is also possible to have different colours for different occasion, season etc. but with limited budget colours must be planned carefully.

Personal Colouring: If colours are not chosen carefully, it can make the skin appear dull and pale, shadowed, coarse or pimply. Yellows and purples emphasize a pale, dull complexion with dark circles under the eyes. If your skin is on the fairer side your choice of colours is almost unlimited. If the skin is dark, the warm colours will be more becoming than the cool colours. Subdued red, subdued orange yellow, mustard, beige, wine colour, crème white are best suited. Slightly subdued cool colours in medium values, greys, navy blue and dark green are wearable at times.

In conclusion of this chapter, it is amply clear that colour is one of the most important ingredients of design composition.

CHAPTER 12

CREATION OF DESIGN

Every design incorporates the basic concepts of elements and principles of design and colour which are essential to develop a good structural design. A good textile designer creates designs on the basis of some new design ideas or gets inspired from historical records, books and magazines and from the nature and environment that surrounds him/her **(Refer Plate 4.24)**.

Design as applied to textile fabrics is synonym to pattern, figure or motif, which is repeated at regular intervals either in woven or printed fabric. The type of textile designs could be grouped in form of a natural, geometrical, floral, stylized or abstract pattern.

Naturalistic Motif: The natural motifs are those which are inspired from one's natural surroundings. In this category the size, shape, form, colour and texture of the created motif almost resembles its original form with slight variation **(Refer Plate 4.25)**.

Geometrical Motif: The designs in this case are based on the geometric foundation of lines, shapes and forms, thus having a formal character **(Refer Plate 4.26)**.

Stylized Motif: The design created in this category have their source of inspiration form the natural sources but the actual composition is distorted, exaggerated or simplified to give it a unnatural form. Thus, the term stylized (Refer Figs. 12.1, 12.2).

Fig. 12.1 A stylized motif

Fig. 12.2 A stylized pattern with foliage

Floral Motif: The flora and fauna are most common patterns or designs seen around in textiles and other several objects. These are inspired from flowers and foliage which may be represented in naturalistic, stylized or geometrical forms. Similar made-up is also possible with the bird or animal motifs **(Refer Plate 4.27, 4.28)**.

Abstract Motif: The abstract pattern is an unfigurative design and is the outcome of stylization of the real objects not following the basic principle of art and design. It consists of unrealistic shapes and irregularities which makes it difficult to identify the design at a first glance **(Refer Plate. 4.29)**.

Thus, by the artistic skill of the textile designers, diverse patterns and motifs could be created for decorating the textiles. This basic unit/motif when repeated all over the length and width of fabric through weaving and printing process changes the design effect produced on the surface of the fabric **(Refer Plate 4.30)**.

A unique design composition with varied effects could be created through placement and appearance of a motif or a pattern in different repeat units.

The various kinds of repeats are:

1. **Straight Repeat:** The design repeats exactly in the same way **(Refer Plate 4.31)**.
2. **Horizontal Mirror Repeat:** The design makes a mirror repeat in the horizontal direction **(Refer Plate 4.32)**.
3. **Vertical Mirror Repeat:** The design makes a mirror repeat in the vertical direction **(Refer Plate 4.33)**.
4. **Rotational Mirror Repeat:** The design forms a mirror repeat both horizontally and vertically making a full circle of 360 degree **(Refer Plate 4.34)**.
5. **Vertical Half Drop Repeat:** Half drop repeat is also called brick repeat. Here the designs are arranged like bricks in a vertical direction **(Refer Plate 4.35)**.
6. **Horizontal Half Drop Repeat:** Here the designs are arranged like bricks in a horizontal fashion **(Refer Plate 4.36)**.

Thus, when a design will reappear on the fabrics forming different repeat patterns it would create varied styles and effects on the fabric surface **(Refer Plate 4.37)**.

ROLE AND IMPORTANCE OF COMPUTERS IN TEXTILE DESIGN

Although the skill of designing is quite multifaceted, it requires the designer to understand its basic principles, elements and concepts to produce varied patterns, colour ways and styles for textile and apparel market which constantly demands changes and innovations.

The traditional way of designing involves creating of patterns on an ivory/cartridge sheet or a point paper, which is an elaborate process and is tedious, time consuming and expensive. And further design on the paper does not have enough clarity and simulation of the actual pattern, its repeat and placement sequence (etc). However, due to the requirement of speedier introduction of new designs in textile market place in today's era, the need for rapid data collection, and continuous design evaluation and innovation becomes immensely important.

With the introduction of various design softwares such as **Paint brush, Photoshop, Illustrator, Auto CAD, Corel Draw,** flexibility in design creation and development is possible with a greater speed and efficiency. It provides a wide spectra to meet the changing demands of consumers and manufacturers **(Refer Plate 4.38, 4.39)**. Therefore, considering the various advantages of digital designing over manual design creation, the designers in the field of textile design have adopted these software tools and strategies not only in the area of designing the prints and patterns but are also being applied to create novel yarns, weave structures and colour concepts.

Thus, computer aided designing provides a tool to a textile designer to enhance his imaginative power and creativity with added features of speedier quality output, and reduction on cost, time and labour.

CONTEMPORARY TEXTILES

Section V

Learning objectives:

By the end of this section the reader would be rendered with the following technical information on:

- A new textile world with recent evolutions of techno textiles having its application in structural and reinforcing components.
- A venture into the world of organic textiles with natural minor fibres like Hemp, Banana, Jute, Linen taking lead to create a eco-friendly version of textile.
- A case study involved Banana fibres usages for apparel purpose: its research and findings.

CHAPTER 13

TECHNO TEXTILES TO ORGANIC/GREEN TEXTILES

Discovery of regenerating natural cellulosic polymer in the form of filaments remains a landmark in the evolution of modern day textiles which revolutionized the textile industry. Before these developments, technology was mainly used to convert natural fibres such as cotton, wool, silk and some quantities of plant fibres into fabrics and garments.

But more recently in world of new textiles, the technological advancements are making a tremendous impact with their look, handle and performance. In the 1990's momentous advances in the technology have provided the field of textiles with the futuristic fabrics that are totally functional as well as beautiful. Thus, the term **"techno textiles"** has emerged which includes the new range of microfibres combined with the unusual mixtures of yarn and fabric textures and incorporating latest weaving, printing, dyeing and finishing technologies. The designers have started to combine these new materials with the traditional fabrics thus creating a new range of fusion textiles.

The future for textiles looks very exciting as the large textile companies are entertaining extensive research, development and innovation in the field of fibre technology. The future fabrics developed will have specific function, such as screening from ultra-violet rays and releasing vitamins into our skin, or fabrics absorbing and reflecting light. Some other examples of techno fabrics are those created with variations in their construction techniques or using diverse materials, such as metals and paper in combination with polyesters and silks, or combining latest micro fibre fabrics with revolutionary methods of printing and newly developed inks, including "retroflective" ink **(Refer Plate 5.1)**. Thus, the textiles are being revolutionized in function, feel and look. However, although the techno textiles have significantly advanced the field of textile designing, the experts in the field feel that these textiles have also brought with them the danger of environmental degradation and pollution hazard. Therefore the current emerging trend is that of a migration towards **organic and eco-friendly textiles.**

Since cotton and plant fibres are grown on land as crop, and wool and silk are animal fibres, there is limitation of quantitative growth of these fibres to meet the demand of ever-growing population of the globe. The manmade fibres thus produced in the factories, are able to meet the demands of the exploding population. But since the synthetic fibres are derived from non-renewable sources based on hydrocarbons such as petroleum and fossil fuels and increasing reliance on these sources is putting a strain on the planet and is not sustainable.

These fibres have the biggest disadvantage of being non-eco-friendly in nature due to its detrimental production and processing techniques which is of great concern to the environmentalist. However, natural fibres have their merit and their production has to be sustained for ecological advantages and for future generation. Therefore, simultaneously, scientific principles are being employed for increasing the yield of cotton per hectare and improving the quality of cotton fibre. Scientific researches are also going on at various organizations in the world to improve the yield and quality of wool and silk fibres. Successful efforts have been made to impart most of the favorable properties of natural fibres to manmade fibres and vice-versa. Since each class of fibres have its own specific functional, aesthetic and economical merits for utmost interest to the consumer, manufacturers want to harness advantages of both **(Refer Plate 5.2)**. Apart from the merits and demerits of the various technologies used to produce the textiles, the major focus in the present times is on Eco-friendly versions. Therefore, there is a paradigm shift to organic farming to produce organic textiles with following principle ideas:

- Soil fertility is maintained or improved by natural methods.
- No use of synthetic pesticides.

Thus, organic textiles which are more recently also termed as **"Green Textiles"** are made from raw materials grown without the use of synthetic chemical fertilisers, pesticides, growth regulators or defoliants.

Cotton is often described as the "Natural Fibre". However, due to its predisposition to insect attacks, conventionally grown cotton uses a high level of chemicals and pesticides. According to PAN UK (Pesticide Action Network) cotton accounts for 10% of all pesticides and 22.5% of insecticides applied in agriculture. It takes 1/3 of a pound of pesticides to produce a tee shirt. The high level of pesticides and insecticides is of major concerns for farmers, wildlife and groundwater. Therefore the cotton producers to a major extent have shifted to growing of organic cotton or green cotton. Apart from cotton fibre, the textile researchers have also ventured into organically producing various other minor fibres like hemp, ramie, wool, linen, banana etc., and thus harnessing the advantage of their eco-friendly characteristics.

Now let us take note of the specific features of each of these green fibres, which are although are extinct in nature and are not newly invented, but still have come into the picture of textiles lately due to the great stress on eco-friendly or organic fibres in order to save the deteriorating environment.

- Hemp has been grown since as early as 800 BC and is used for a variety of purposes. Its applications in food, animal feed, cosmetics and toiletries, biofuel, textiles, biodegradable plastic, paper etc. It is present throughout the history of civilization, from the Magna Carta to the US Declaration of Independence, both of which were drafted on hemp paper.

  Hemp sheds many of its leaves before harvest, thus returning nutrients to the soil for the next crop. It is also fairly disease free if kept in a proper crop rotation scheme. So from many points of view, hemp seems to be an ideal candidate for organic textile production **(Refer Plate 5.3)**.

  Organic hemp could very well replace conventional cotton in the production of textiles and could increase the share of organic textiles in total textile production. As hemp can grow to 5 meters and provides a high yield of fibre, this crop could certainly provide the textile industry with ample raw materials.

- Organic wool has all the good qualities of conventionally produced wool while having the added advantage of being produced in a sustainable and ethical way. There are up to 8,000 different chemicals that exist in non-organic wool, causing allergies, rashes, and itchiness. Organic wool is free of pesticides, formaldehyde, polyester, foams, dioxins and other additives used in conventional manufacturing practices. Bio Gro certification for merino wool also ensures that responsible animal practices are used.

- Valued for its strength and durability linen, like hemp, has been cultivated for thousand of years. Linen is strong, durable and absorbs moisture. Its permeability and heat conductivity properties make linen ideal for any situation. Linen is obtained from the flax plant. Flax plants grow with very little to no pesticides, making linen a sustainable alternative to cotton. As a bi-product flax seed oil is very valuable and is used in paint (linseed oil) and in food. In hot weather linen clothes will keep you cool while in cold weather they will keep you warm.

  While conventional linen is already a highly sustainable crop, organic linen is grown according to high ecological standards without the use of synthetic substances, while promoting crop rotations. This helps preserve biodiversity and encourage sustainability.

Thus, to be precise, all green fibres referred to as organic are guaranteed to have come from crops or livestock inspected and certified by institutions recognized by the International Federation of Organic Agricultural Movements (IFOAM), which certifies the organic produce, which has been controlled through the entire production cycle. Certification of textiles is based on 2 principles: (1) all fibres must be natural and grown in an organic manner, (2) the whole process should be taken into account, which means every processing step (spinning, weaving, washing, etc.), has to meet certain criteria which are set to be environmentally responsible. Also, green fibres clothes do not receive any synthetic chemical finishes or treatments (e.g. moth resistant, fire retardant, easy care, anti pilling, etc.). All dyes used on green fibres clothing are either plant or mineral derived, or if not of natural origin, are environmentally responsible low impact dyes. No heavy metals or other harmful chemicals are used in the dyeing process. Additional social criteria also ensure minimum standards applied to working conditions.

Thus, natural fibres such as hemp and linen, as well as organic cotton and wool, are produced without harming the environment. They also provide real ecological solutions to the draining of the earth's resources. An ethically and environmentally aware approach is extended for organically grown produce using bio-dynamic methods. 'Green' textile and fashion products have appeared in designer collections and exclusive fashion stores **(Plate 5.4)**.

Constant researches are being carried out in order to cater to green factor in the field of clothing and textiles. One such case study in the field is presented in the following text for you review.

CHAPTER 14

CASE STUDY ON ECO-TEXTILES (Banana Fibres)

AN EXPERIMENTAL STUDY ON CREATING SUITABLE FABRICS FOR APPAREL PURPOSE USING BANANA FIBRES

In the environmental conscious world today, the banana fibres can be immensely friendly, as the products merges with the soil after sustained use. Banana is cultivated in larger section of land in the country. The stems after harvesting of the fruits if properly exploited, would lead to harnessing the huge agricultural waste to economic advantage.

Certain promotional steps of utilizing banana fibres for making of fancy items like bags, table mats, purses by plaiting techniques has already begin carried out. The potential of using banana fibre for textile applications has been recognized by KVIC, which has been trying to improve the present conditions of natural fibres in order to upgrade quality of fibre, to improve extraction methods and is even conducting research to improve the wear characteristics of the banana fibre.

Weaving of fabric from pineapple fibres is already being carried out at SITRA, Coimbatore. Pineapple and banana have similar properties and functionalism, both being a leaf fibre. Thus, a research idea of weaving of fabric from banana fibre could also be experimented. This lead the way for the present study conducted on creating suitable fabrics for apparel purpose using banana fibres.

Making of unique fabric and converting it into a designer wear is an important aspect. In this study designer fabrics were created using variation in designs, yarns and weaves which lead to the creation of fabrics with a variety and added a new look to the overall appearance of the apparels constructed.

Silky lusture, tolerable tensile strength, low extensibility, high stiffness, long staple lengths are some of the inherent properties of banana fibres. Exploring the banana fibre to still greater extent and blending of banana with costlier natural and synthetic fibres like cotton, rayon, nylon etc., can overcome certain inherent deficiencies like coarseness, brittleness and harshness in feel, feel appearance, stiffness, inextensibility etc., and add a number of features like novel dyeing effects, better eye appeal, washability, durability and reduced fibre shedding.

This study deals with the creation of fabrics for apparel purpose from banana fibres and evaluating their suitability. With the growing awareness towards environmental trends and a shift in demand for bio-degradable product, a range of apparels was designed from banana fabric. This research which in turn could benefit both the banana cultivators and weaver's gainful employment was carried upon with following objectives:

Objectives of the Study

1. To study the feasibility of making yarns from banana fibres for weaving.
2. To study the effects created due to different placement of warps i.e., denting order.
3. To know the effect created by use of filling yarns of different thickness and nature.
4. To analyze the banana fabric for different properties.
5. Designing and construction of suitable value added apparels from the woven fabrics.
6. To evaluate the preferences and acceptability of the designed apparels.

Limitations of the Study

1. Two harness table loom was used.
2. Limited apparel products for exclusive wear that is Jackets, Yokes and Tops were designed woven and constructed.
3. Denting order of 17 inches and 34 inches was used.

Initially the feasibility of blending cotton with banana fibres; spinning and making yarns on cotton spinning system was tried. Since it was not possible to spin yarns from banana fibres it was decided to use cotton and rayon as warp yarns and banana fibres as weft with different characteristics.

Three sets of apparels were designed, woven and constructed Set – I Jackets, Set – II Tops and Set – III Yokes. The warp yarns used were of 2/10s unbleached, non-mercerized cotton yarn for Set I and II and delustured rayon yarns for were used Set III.

The warps were dyed with cold reactive dyes according to the design prior to threading and wefts were also dyed with direct dyes before weaving. For attaining a unique textural appearance of the fabric woven, weft yarns (banana fibres) of different thicknesses and nature were created. The variations in both yarn and weave were carried out. Yarn variations was brought about by using weft as:

(i) Banana fibre strands

(ii) Through weaver's knot.

(iii) Yarn tyeing and dyeing.

(iv) Ply yarn.

(v) Plaited yarn.

While weave and textural was done by quilting and incorporating weaving techniques –

(i) Tapestry technique

(ii) Figure weaving.

(iii) Basket weave.

Fifty respondents gave their opinions. Questionnaire was scheduled and the apparels were ranked for their design and suitability **(Refer Plate 5.5)**.

Analysis of the woven Banana fabric for different properties

Fabrics woven with different warp sets having weft has 5-7 strands of banana fibre were considered for testing for different properties like percent count, weight per unit area, fabric thickness, tensile strength, stiffness and abrasion resistance to roughly estimate the serviceability of the banana fabrics.

The weight per unit area and fabric thickness was more in case where cotton yarns were used as warps, compared to rayon ones in the banana fabric.

The banana fibre strands in weft being stiffer and non-flexible also tend to increase thickness. The tenacity values obtained by the banana cotton fabric were within the tolerable limits as compared to other cellulosic fibres. The stiffness values indicate that banana fabric can be graded as a fairly stiff fabric. This aspect should be taken into consideration by the designer in construction of garments. Abrasion resistance of banana fabric is quite favourable. The fabric construction in this case was such that only cotton yarns get abraded and the weft yarns remained resistant to abrasion. The weft though present on the surface of the fabric, did not tend to abrade. Distortion was observed due to the presence of looseness of weave. Lastly the laundering of banana fabric showed that a minimal loss in stiffness, and shrinkage also occurred to some extent.

All these results bring forth the fact that the banana fibres can be effectively used and could be well utilized for exclusive apparel purpose with further researches, this study would diversify the use of banana fibres, if used as a fabric for apparel construction.

The banana fibres being cheaper, and having utilization of the waste it can be turned out as "Best out of waste".

Thus, optimum utilization of the banana fibres should be done for the development of handloom banana fabrics. The banana fabric is value based, giving employment opportunity particularly to rural population.

Today, banana should be looked upon as a textile fibre, which helps to protect the environment and maintain ecological balance in the era of "green cotton".

RECOMMENDATIONS

1. A study could be carried out on spinning of banana with other fibres on jute spinning machinery.
2. A study could be carried out on improving the tensile strength of banana fibres.
3. A study could be carried out on reduction of stiffness of banana fibres.
4. A study related to printing of banana fabrics could be carried out.

On a concluding note, textile design looks at fibre blends, fabric weaves, colour, pattern and finishing types. Designers explore techniques to create new patterns, new hand and finishing processes for a product. Environmental issues will make designing much more complex because it requires a more thorough knowledge of production processes than ever before. Some of the major problems are due to the complexities of the textile processing chain. Understanding the impacts of raw materials, use of chemical substances, processing and production methods requires a high degree of technical knowledge, as a result research is underway to find solutions that are technically, economically and environmentally feasible. Collective approaches are therefore required on the part of manufacturers and consumers to adopt these organic textiles to facilitate environmental protection.

APPENDIX I

CAREERS IN THE FIELD OF TEXTILE DESIGN

Below is a list of representative careers in the field of textile design at entry level:

I. Stylist	*II. Designer*	*III. Computer Designer/Artist*	*IV. Management Field*	*V. Miscellaneous*
Textile Stylist	Assistant Designer	CAD/CAM Designer	Management Trainee	Textile Technologist
Menswear Stylist	Sweater Designer	CAD Designer/ Editor	Marketing Representative	Textile Conservation
Womenswear Stylist	Design Assistant	Freelance Artist	Design Salesperson	Quality Assurance
Assistant Stylist	Tie/Print Designer	Textile Artist	Sales Engineer	Knitting Machine Operator
Stylist Jacquard	Design Trainee	Graphic Artist	Sales Consultant	Fabric Development Specialist
Fabric Stylist	Jacquard Design Assistant	CAD Artist	Marketing Manager	Free Lance Designer
Interior Stylist	Assistant to Knitwear Designer	Sketcher	New Product Development	Textile Trainee
	Lace Designer	CAD Operator	Product Development Designer	Sample Maker

I. Stylist	*II. Designer*	*III. Computer Designer/Artist*	*IV. Management Field*	*V. Miscellaneous*
	Print Designer	CAD Technician	Sales Consultant/ Leather	Self-employed Handweaver
	Technical Designer		Operations Research Analyst	
	Assistant Print Designer		Quality Controller	
	Design Technician			
	Assistant Textile Designer			
	Design Editor			

APPENDIX II

LIST OF RELEVANT RESOURCES IN THE FIELD OF TEXTILE DESIGN

Below is a list of resources in the field of textile design, which will help the students and researchers to obtain relevant information for their advanced career development.

I. Institutions

- J.D. Institute of Fashion Design – J.D. Hemu Arcade, Opp. Vileparle Station (W) Mumbai
- J.D. Fashion Institute – http://www.jdinstitute.com
- National Institute of Fashion Technology – Established in 1987 in Delhi, it is now spread over 7 cities of India
- National Institute of Design (NID) – Paldi, Ahmedabad – 380007
- National Institute of Fashion Design – First opened at Chandigarh in 1995; since then it has opened more than 80 franchises over the country
- Fashion Institute of Design and Merchandising – FIDM is a private institute with its other centers in the US. It has its institutes at San Francisco, San Diego, Los Angeles and Orange County, California.
- Premila Vithaldas Polytechnic – S. N. D. T. Juhu Tara Road, Santacruz (W), Mumbai–400049

- Sophia Polytechnic – Bhulabhai Desai Road, Breach Candy, Mumbai–400027
- L. S. Raheja Technical Institute – Adarsh Nagar, Worli, Mumbai–400018
- DEI Women's Polytechnic, Technical College, Dayalbagh, Agra–282005

II. Courses

- Textile and Apparel Design
- Fashion Design
- Textile Designing
- Fashion Merchandise Marketing
- Graphic Design
- Visual Communications
- Export Marketing of Textiles
- CAD/CAM in Textiles
- Printing Design

III. Magazines

- ABCD Lady
- Elite
- Elle Now
- Femina
- Hurleys
- Images Fashion
- Inflight reading magazines; swagat, jetwings etc.
- Saavy

IV. Retailers

- Fab India
- Hide Design
- Nalli
- Pantaloon
- Raymond
- Shoppers Stop
- Westside

V. Organisations

- Ministry of Textiles, Govt. of India

- Coir Board
- Cotton Textile Council of India
- Fashion Design Council of India (FDCI)
- Handlooms Development Commissioner
- Khadi and Village Industries Commission
- Leather Export Council
- National Centre for Textile Design (NCTD)
- Silk-Central Board
- Silk Indian Export Promotion Council
- Jute Manufacturers Development Council
- Jute Manufacturers Export Council
- Jute National Centre
- Powerloom Export Promotion Council
- Textiles Committee

VI. Public Sector Undertakings

- National Textile Corporation Ltd., New Delhi.
- British India Corporation, Kanpur.
- Cotton Corporation of India Ltd., Mumbai.
- Jute Corporation of India Ltd., Calcutta.
- Birds, Jute and Exports Ltd., Calcutta.
- National Jute Manufacturers Corporation, Calcutta.
- Handicrafts and Handlooms Export Corporation, New Delhi.
- Central Cottage Industries Corporation, New Delhi.
- North-Eastern Handicrafts and handlooms Development Corporation, Shillong.
- National Handloom Development Corporation, Lucknow.

VII. Textile Research Associations

- Ahmedabad Textile Industry Research Association, Ahmedabad.
- Bombay Textile Research Association, Mumbai.
- South India Textile Research Association, Coimbatore.
- Northern India Textile Research Association, Ghaziabad.
- Silk and Art Silk Mills Research Association, Mumbai.
- Manmade Textile Research Association, Surat.

- Indian Jute Industry's Research Association, Calcutta.
- Wool Research Association, Thane.

VIII. Export Promotion Councils

- Handloom Export Promotion Council, Chennai.
- Handicrafts and Handlooms Export Corporation (HHEC)
- Apparel Export Promotion Council, New Delhi.
- Cotton Textile Export Promotion Council, Mumbai.
- The Silk and Rayon Textile Export Promotion Council, Mumbai.
- Indian Silk Export Promotion Council, New Delhi.
- Wool and Woollen Export Promotion Council, New Delhi.
- Carpet Export Promotion Council, New Delhi.
- Export Promotion Council for Handicrafts, New Delhi.
- Powerloom Development and Export Promotion Council, Mumbai.

IX. Advisory Bodies

- Cotton Advisory Board.
- Jute Advisory Board.
- Development Council for Textile Industry.
- Co-ordination Council for Textile Research Associations.
- Jute Manufacturers Development Council.
- All India Handloom Board.
- All India Handicrafts Board.
- All India Powerloom Board.
- Nodal Agency for Sick Textile Mills.

X. Autonomous Bodies

- Textiles Committee, Mumbai.
- Wool Development Board, Jodhpur.
- National Institute of Fashion Technology, New Delhi.
- National Centre for Jute Diversification, Calcutta.

XI. Commodity Board

- Central Silk Board, Bangalore.

APPENDIX III

LIST OF POSSIBLE RESEARCH TOPICS IN THE FIELD OF TEXTILE DESIGN

Below is a list of possible and emerging research project topics in the field of textile design, which will provide the aspiring researchers and PhD scholars a glimpse of research possibilities in this area:

- Historical perspective of traditional textiles in India.
- Chemical and physical properties of newer and eco-friendly fibres.
- Feasibility analysis of techno-textiles.
- Feasibility analysis of green textiles.
- Environmental aspects of textile designing.
- Designing aspects of effluent treatment for textile industry.
- Colour trends in textile and clothing industry.
- Fashion Forecasting in textile and clothing industry.
- The role of influencers and innovators in textile new product development.
- Use of collaborative editing and designing systems in textile new product development.
- Design and application of composite materials in textile designing.
- Comparative analysis of different traditional textiles development from different parts of India.
- Comparative analysis of Indian and Western textiles.

BIBLIOGRAPHY

SELECTED REFERENCES

1. Corbman Bernard P., Textiles Fibre to Fabric, McGraw–Hill Book Co., 1985.
2. Dantyagi Susheela, Fundamentals of Textiles and their Care, Orient Longman Ltd., New Delhi, 1984.
3. D' Souza Noemia, Fabric Care, New Age International (P) Ltd. Publishers, New Delhi, 1988.
4. Hess K.P., Textiles, Fibres and their use, New Delhi, Oxford and IPHP Publishing Co., 1966.
5. Joseph Majory L., Introductory Textile Science, Holt, Rinehart and Winston, Inc., 1966.
6. Marsh J. T., Textile Science – An introductory Manual, B.I. Publications, Delhi, 1948.
7. Pandit S. and Trarpley E., Grooming, Selection and Care of Clothes, Savitri Pandit, Clothing and Textiles Department Faculty of Home Science, M.S. University, Baroda, 1975.
8. Sreenivasan Murthy H.V., Introduction to Textile Fibres, The Textile Association India, 1987.
9. Sturm Mary Mark, Corieser Edwina H., Guide to Modern Clothing, Webster Division, McGraw–Hill Book Co., 1962.
10. Watkins D.W., Neely Juanita, South Carolina Extension Service, Clemson Agricultural College, South Carolina.
11. Kadolf Sera, Laugford Anna, 2002, Textiles, Prentice Hall.

12. Gupta Sushma, Garg Neeru, Saini Renu, 1996, Clothing and Textile, Kalyani Publishers.
13. Pannu Gurpreet, 1995, International Standards for Testing Woven and Knitted Fabrics, Department of Textiles and Clothing, Lady Irwin College, Delhi University.
14. Pissuto, Joseph J., 1990, Fabric Science, Fair Child Publications.
15. Langerford Kadolph 1995, Textiles, Prentice Hall.
16. Dantyagi Sushila, 1987, Fundamentals of Textiles and their Care, Orient Longman Ltd., New Delhi.
17. Deular Durga, 1967, Household Textiles & Laundry Work, Atmaram & Sons., New Delhi.

PLATES SECTION—I

Plate 1.1: Modified spinning wheel adapted from the ancient one

Plate 1.2: John Kay shuttle loom 1753

Plate 1.3: Power loom in a mill

Plate 1.4: Rich brocade of Benaras

Plate 1.5: Border of a banarsi saree

Plate 1.6: A auenthetic piece of kanchipuram silk

Plate 1.7: A rich coloured textured kanchipuram

Plate1.8: A floral motif on a paithani saree

Plate 1.9: Motifs in a paithani saree

Plate 1.10: A Baluchar bootidar saree

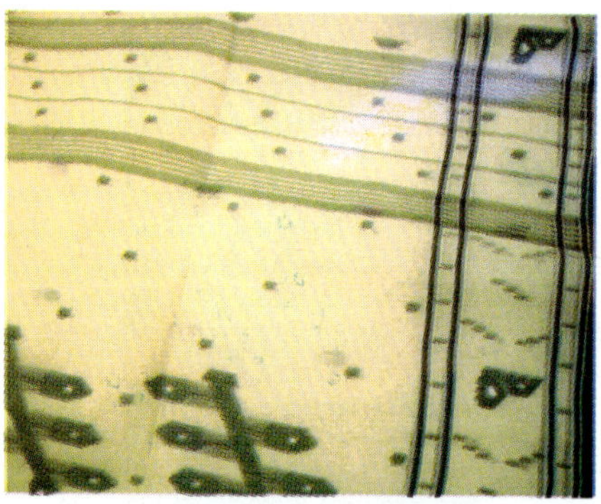

Plate 1.11: Muslin based Jamdhani saree

Plate 1.12: A beutifully patterened and dyed Jamdhani

Plate 1.13: Sanganeri printed fabric

Plate 1.14: A typical sanganeri motif

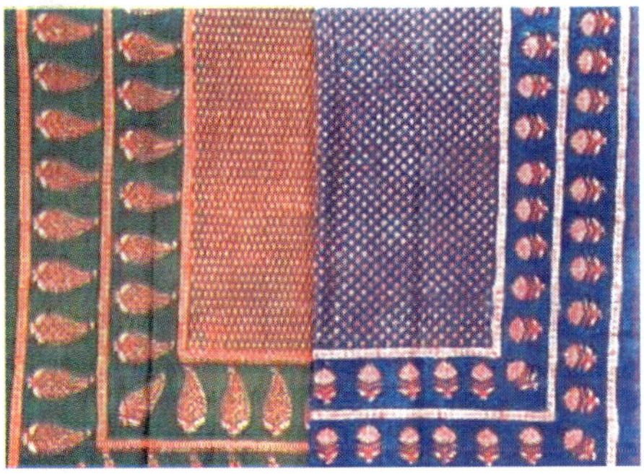

Plate 1.15: Bhagru prints

Plate 1.16: A piece of traditional Kalamkari

Plate 1.17: A Mathila painting
with bright shades

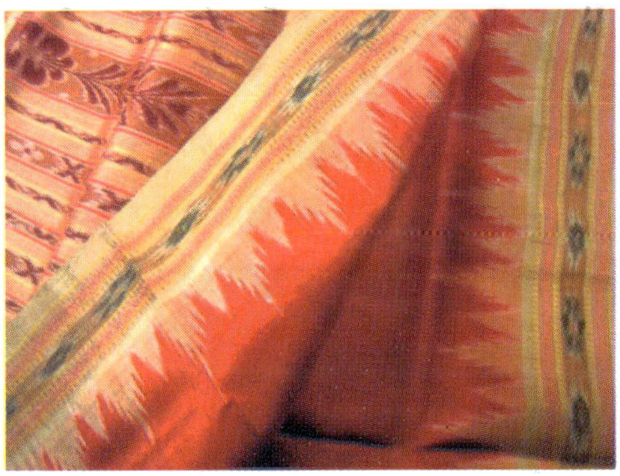

Plate 1.18: Orissa Ikat

Plate 1.19: Mashru fabric from Andhra Pradesh

Plate 1.20: Pochampalli saree

Plate 1.21: A typical motif of bhandani

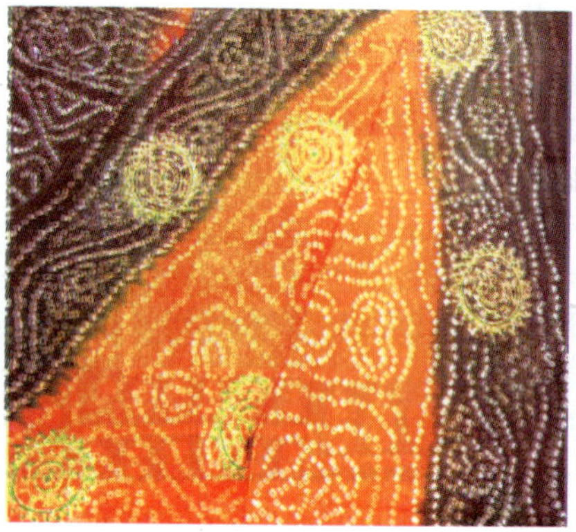

Plate 1.22: A Bhandani saree

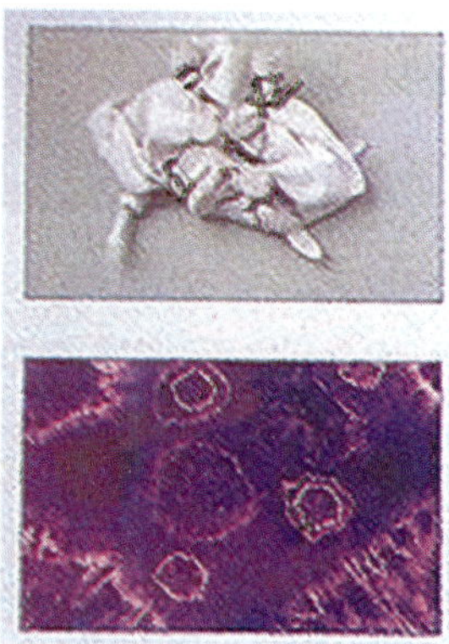

Plate 1.23: Uneven Knotting technique

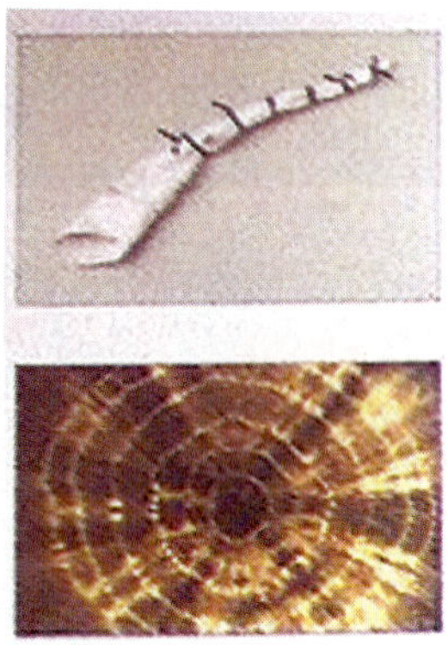

Plate 1.24: Rod/stick tyeing technique

Plate 1.25: Crumpled tyeing technique

Plate 1.26: Tyeing at intervals

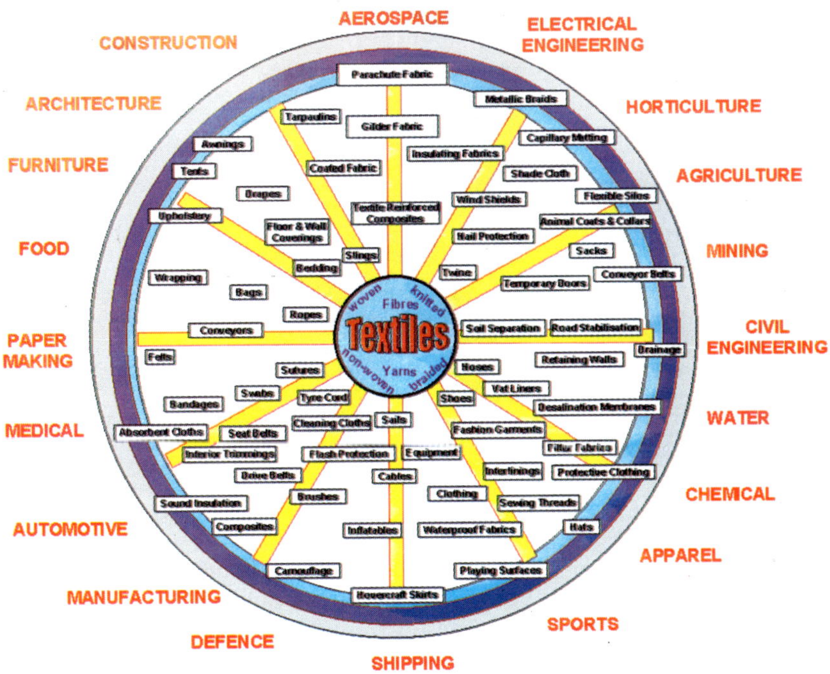

Plate 1.27: Textile wheel

Heat protection

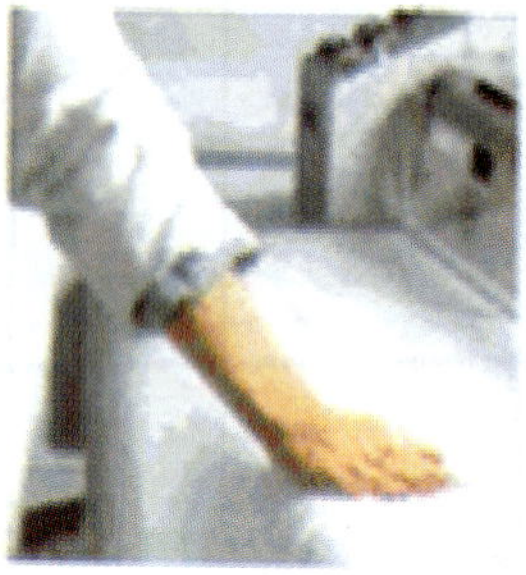

Industry

Filtration

Clothing for Firemen (Firefighters)

Cut protection

Plate 1.28: Versatile applications of textiles

PLATES SECTION—II

CLASSIFICATION OF TEXTILE FIBRES

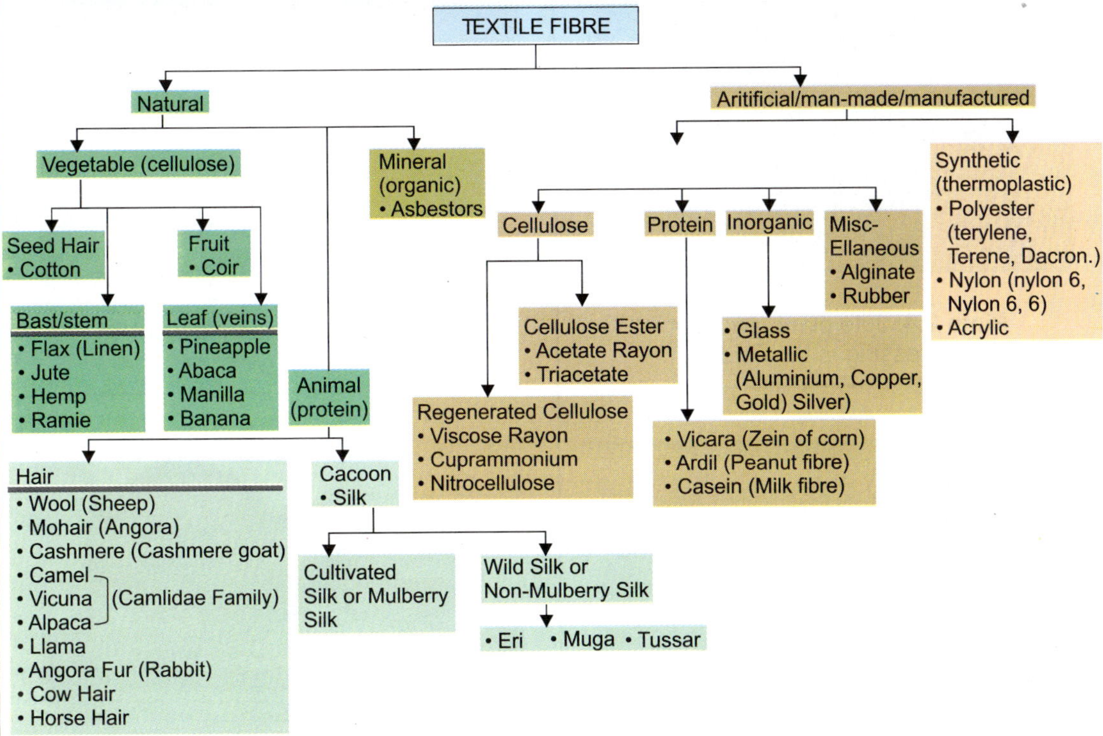

Plate 2.1: A chart showing classification of fibres

Plate 2.2: A cotton plant yielding raw cotton fibre

Plate 2.3: A flax plant

Plate 2.4: Jute plant ready for processing in the fields

Plate 2.5: Shearing wool

Plate 2.6: A silk worm feeding on mulberry leaves

Plate 2.7: Fibres spun and dyed into yarns

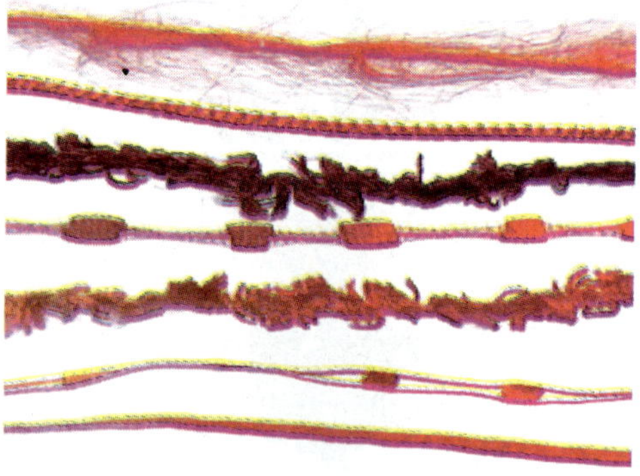

Plate 2.8: A picture showing different novelty yarns

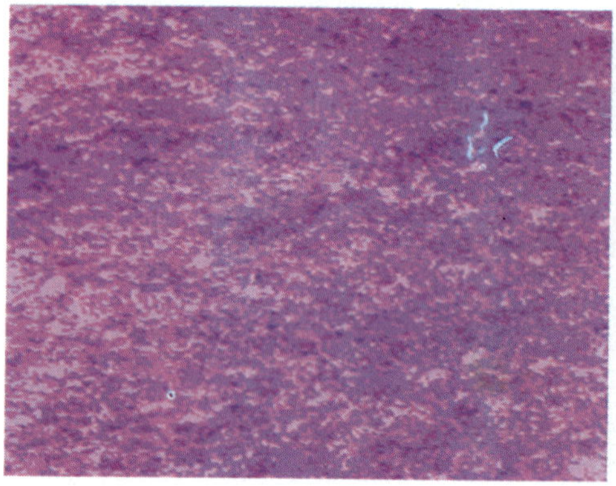

Plate 2.9: Interlocking technique in fibres; Felt

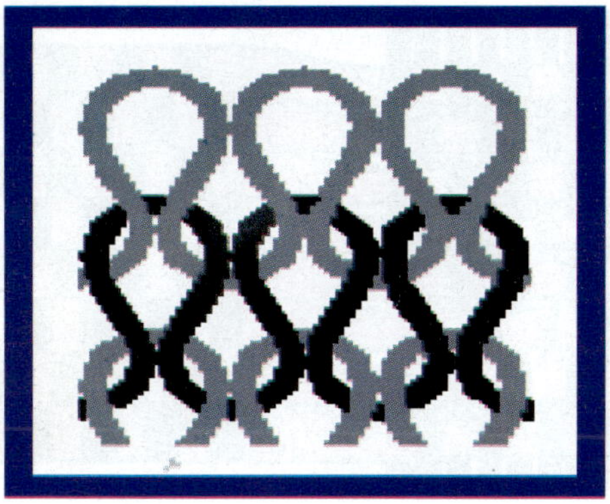

Plate 2.10: Inter looping technique of knitting

Plate 2.11: Interlacing technique of weaving

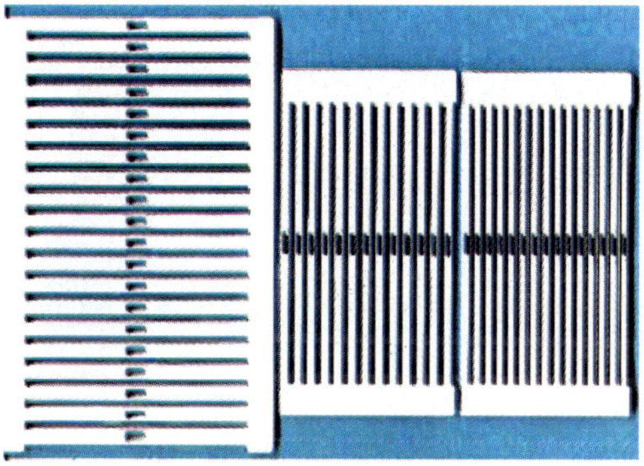

Plate 2.11(a): Headles

Plate 2.12: Reed

Plate 2.13: Shuttle and bobbin for weft yarn

Plate 2.14: Shuttle loom

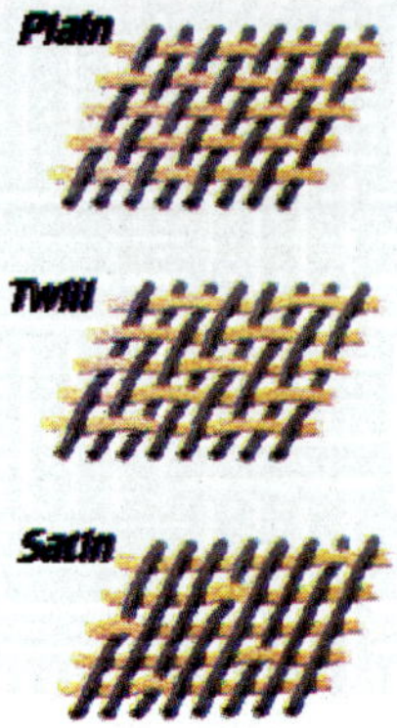

Plate 2.15: Basic ABC weave structures

Plate 2.16: Plain weave structure

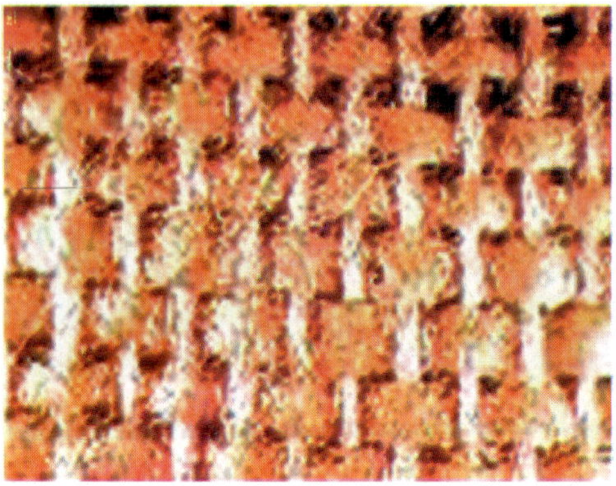

Plate 2.17: Plain woven burlap fabric

Plate 2.18: Chiffon fabric

Plate 2.19: Woven checks in a plain fabric (Gingham)

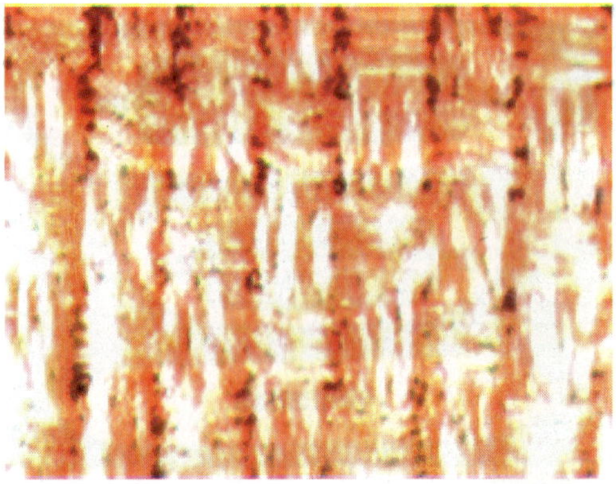

Plate 2.20: Basket weave structure in a monk's cloth

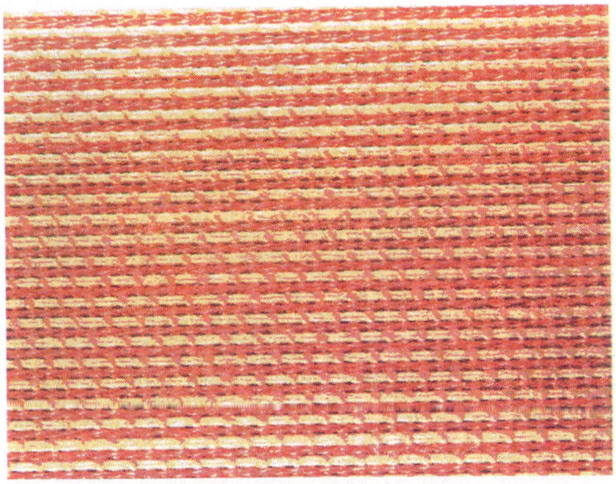

Plate 2.21: Weft Rib weave in a baby cord fabric

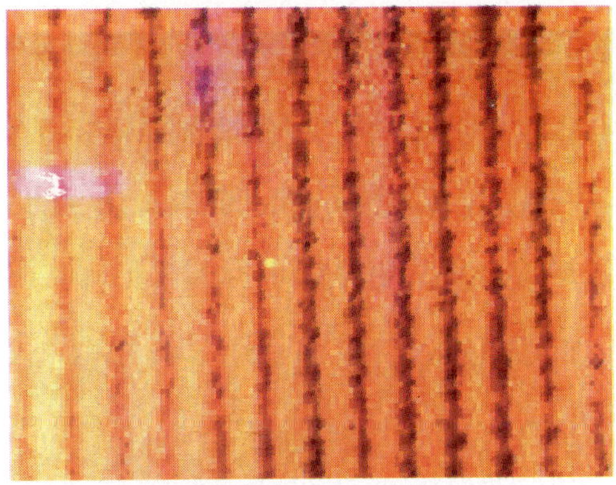

Plate 2.22: Warp Rib structure in a corduroy fabric

Plate 2.23: Twill weave structure

Plate 2.24: Twill weave in a denim fabric

Plate 2.25: Right hand twill structure in a drill fabric

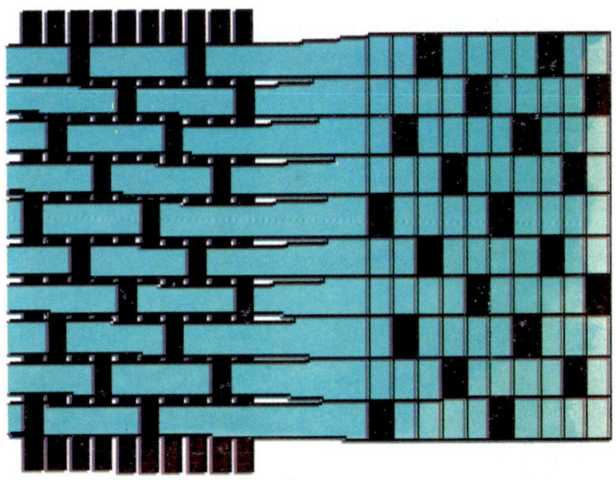

Plate 2.26: Satin weave structure

Plate 2.27: Satin fabric

Plate 2.28: Sateen fabric

Plate 2.29: Dobby loom

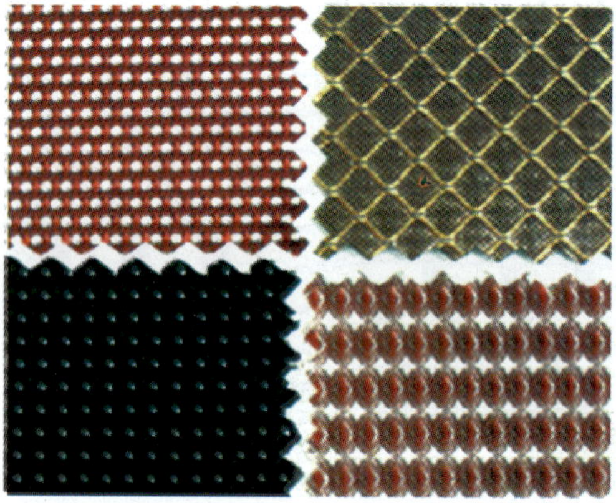

Plate 2.30: Dobby fabrics

Plate 2.31: A full view of Jacquard fabric

Plate 2.32: Jacquard fabric

PLATES SECTION—III

Plate 3.1: Scouring machine

Plate 3.2: Singeing machine with flame below the fabric

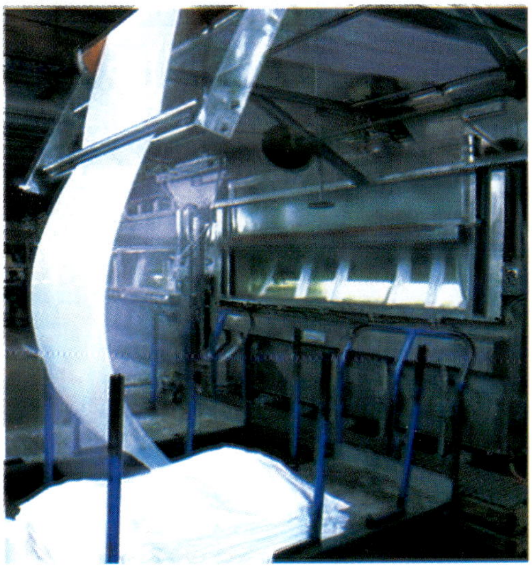

Plate 3.3: A bleaching machine

Plate 3.4: Embossed fabric

Plate 3.5: Napped fabric with protruding short hairs

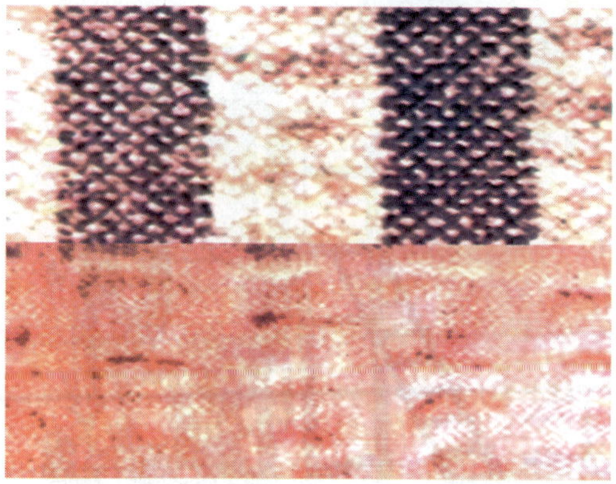

Plate 3.6: Plisse fabric in comparison with Seer sucker fabric

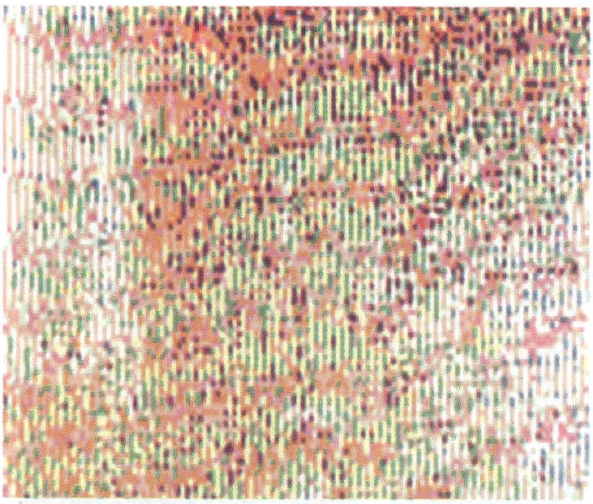

Plate 3.7: Parchementizing finish in a organdy fabric

Plate 3.8: Dyeing Laboratory

Plate 3.9: Bulk dyeing machine

Plate 3.10: Discharge printing through block printing process

Plate 3.11: Lilonium blocks for printing

Plate 3.12: Block Printing Process

Plate 3.13: Block printed fabric

Plate 3.14: Process of screen printing

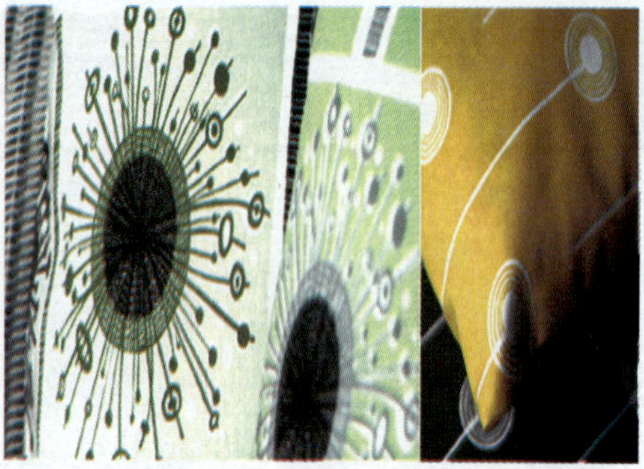

Plate 3.15: Screen prints on furnishings

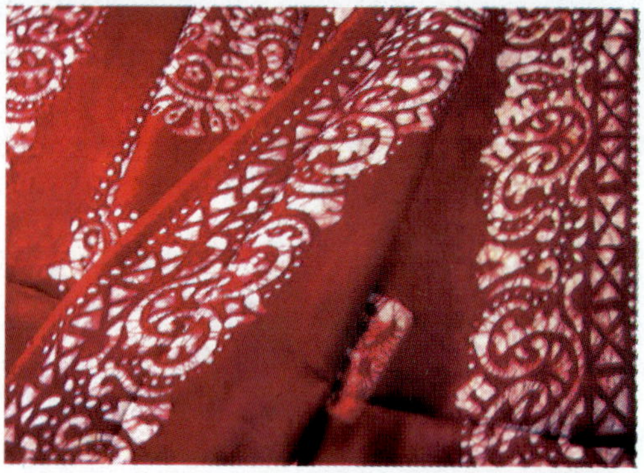

Plate 3.16: Stylized print through batik

Plate 3.17: Sample of batik similar to that of hand painting

Plate 3.18: Tie and dye through resist technique

Plate 3.19: Rotary roller printing

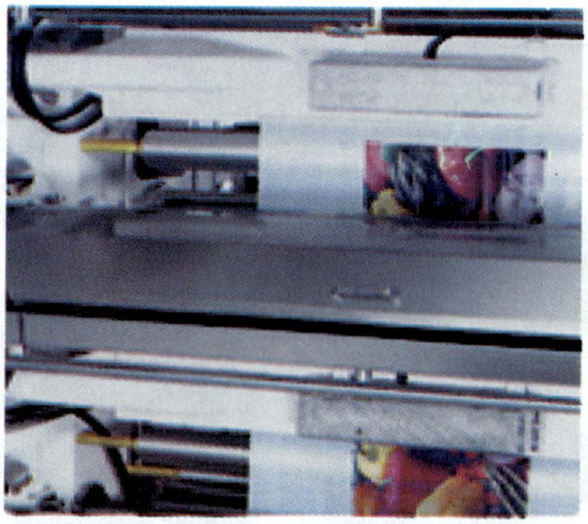

Plate 3.20: Digital printing machine

PLATES SECTION—IV

Plate 4.1: Horizontal lines creating a width in design

Plate 4.2: Verticle lines in a design

Plate 4.3: Curved lines in a pattern

Plate 4.4: Diagonal block pattern in design composition

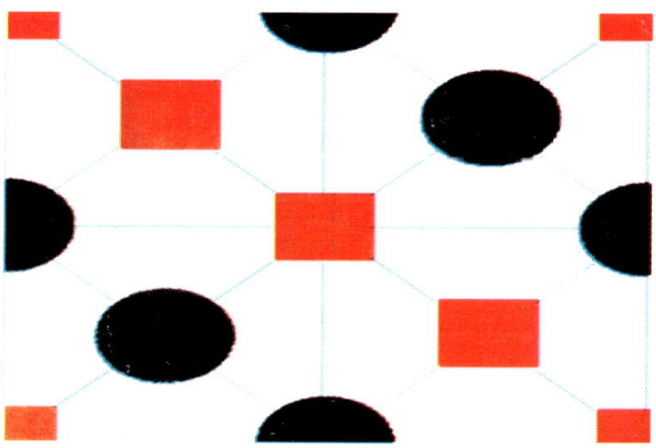

Plate 4.5: White – negative space in a design red and black shapes – positive space

Plate 4.6: Stiff and rough textured fabric

Plate 4.7: Smooth and flowing texture

Plate 4.8: Prisim with its reflective colour rays

Plate 4.9: Chart displaying hue, value & saturation

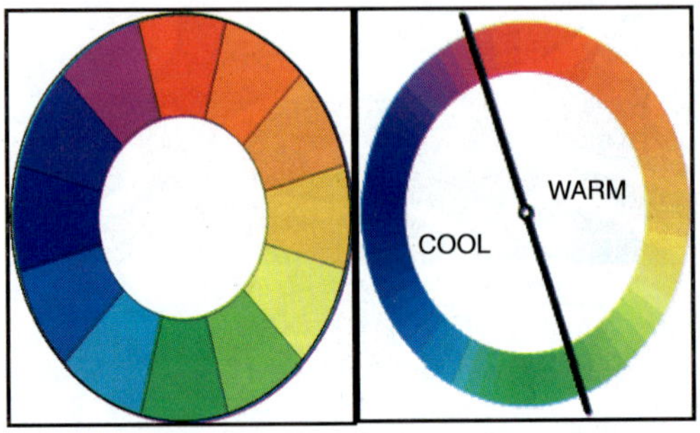

Plate 4.10: Colour wheel with warm and cool colours

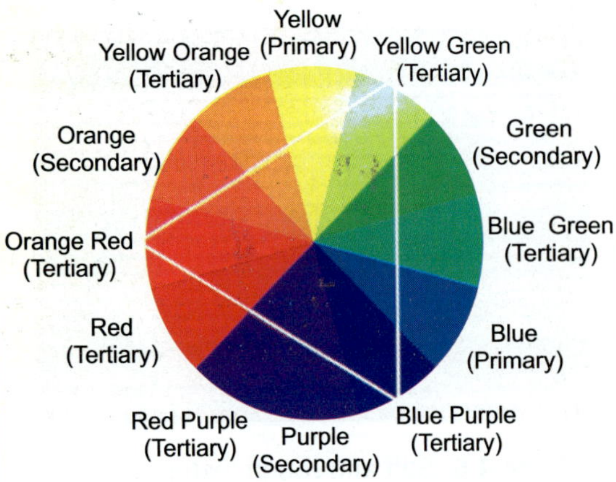

Plate 4.11: Colour wheel

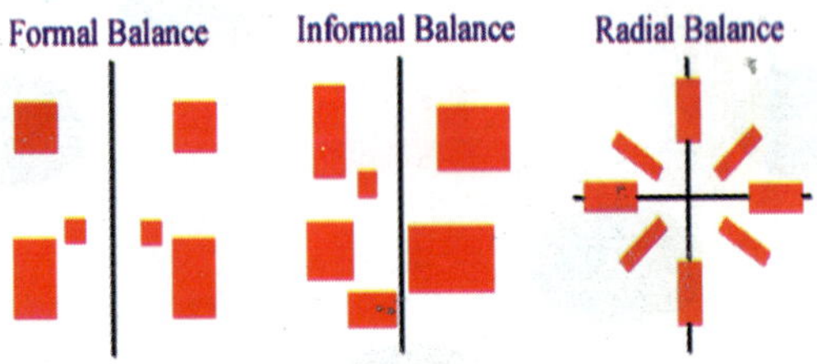

Plate 4.12: Different types of Balance

Plate 4.13: Balance in a design

Plate 4.14: A design with poor proportions

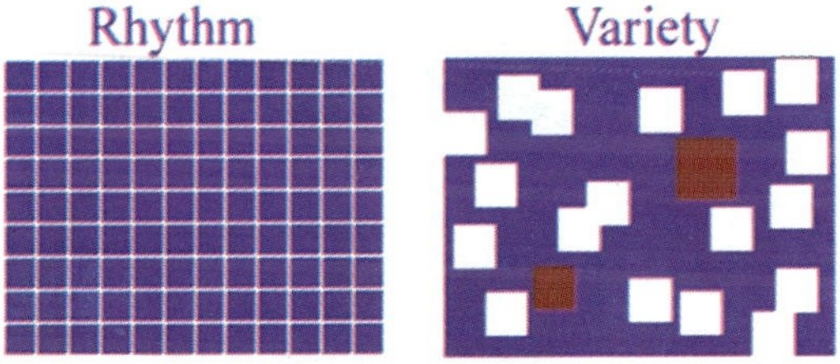

Plate 4.15: Variation in rhythm and variety

Plate 4.16: Flowing rythmic pattern in a design

Plate 4.17: Emphasis in a design

Plate 4.18: Harmony in a design

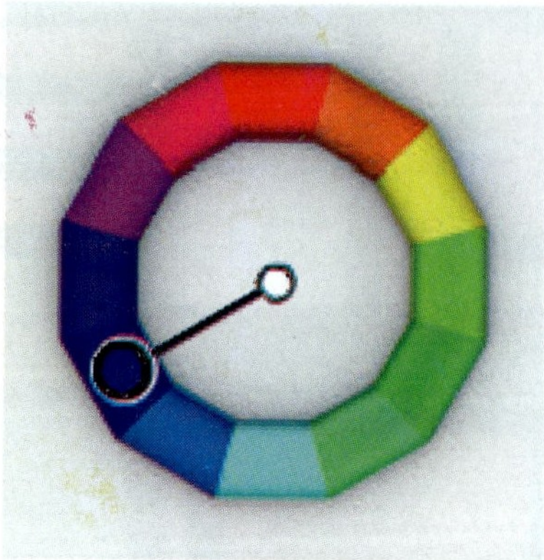

Plate 4.19: Monochromatic colour scheme

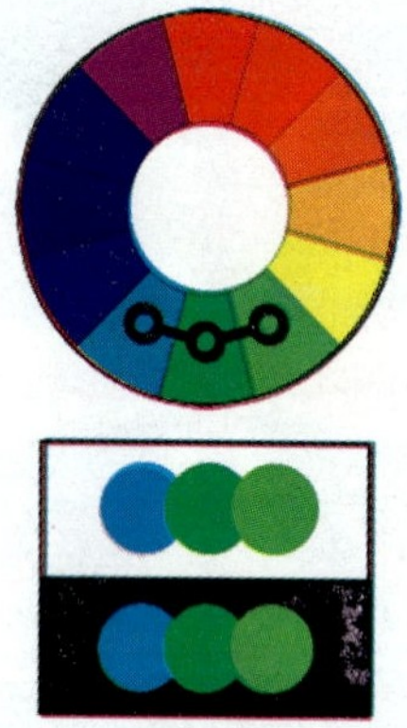

Plate 4.20: Analogous colour harmony

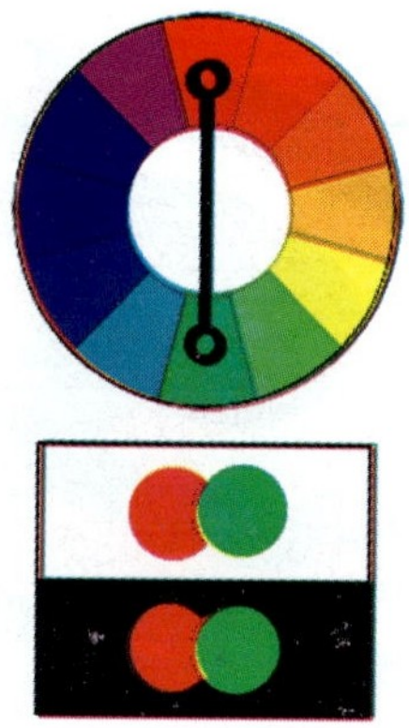

Plate 4.21: Complementary colour scheme

Plate 4.22: Split complementary colour scheme

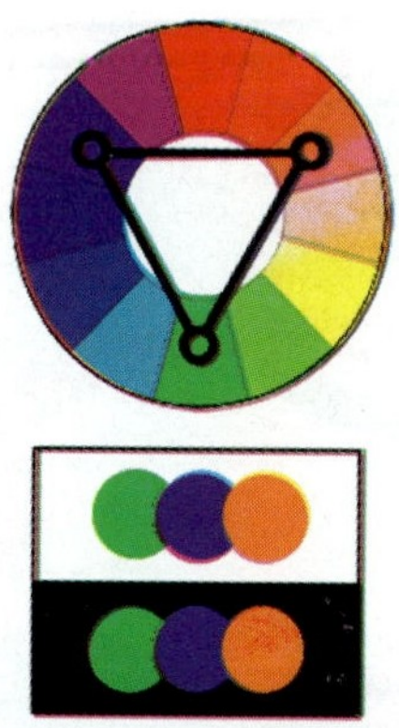

Plate 4.23: Traid colour scheme

Plate 4.24: Naturalistic concept could be adopted as a design

Plate 4.25: Naturalistic motif

Plate 4.26: A simple geometric

Plate 4.27: A typical floral motif

Plate 4.28: A nursery print on a fabric

Plate 4.29: An abstract pattern

Plate 4.30: Combination of lines and shapes in a geometric motif

Plate 4.31: Straight repeat

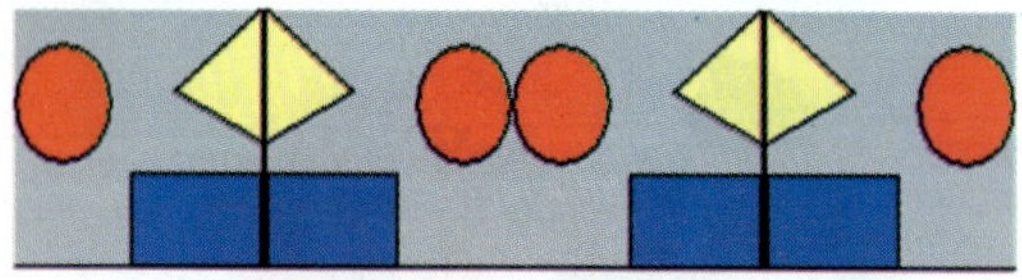

Plate 4.32: Horizontal mirror repeat

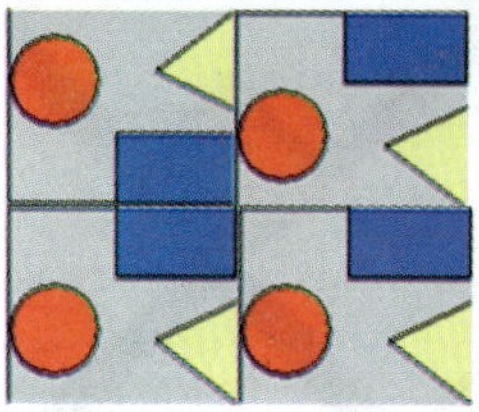

Plate 4.33: Vertical mirror repeat

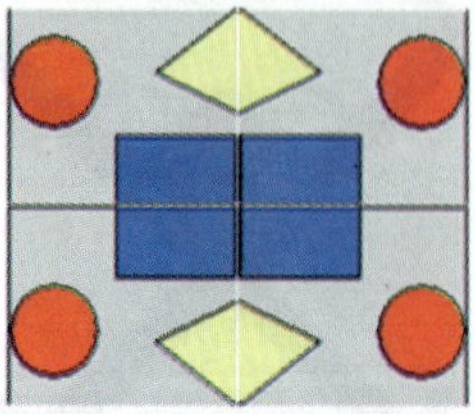

Plate 4.34: Rotational mirror repeat

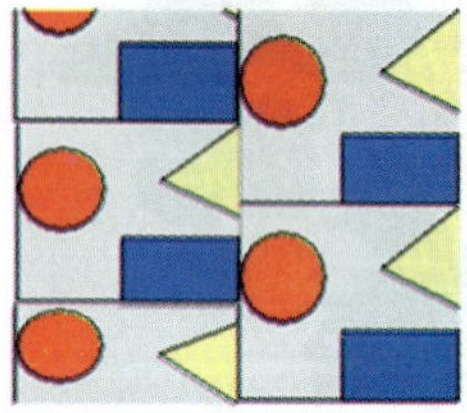

Plate 4.35: Vertical half drop repeat

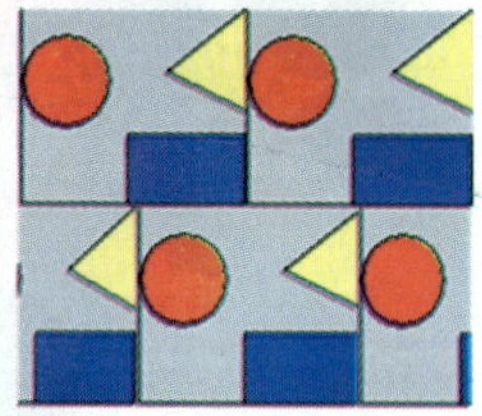

Plate 4.36: Horizontal half drop repeat

Plate 4.37: Some interesting patterns created through use of simple lines, shapes and colours

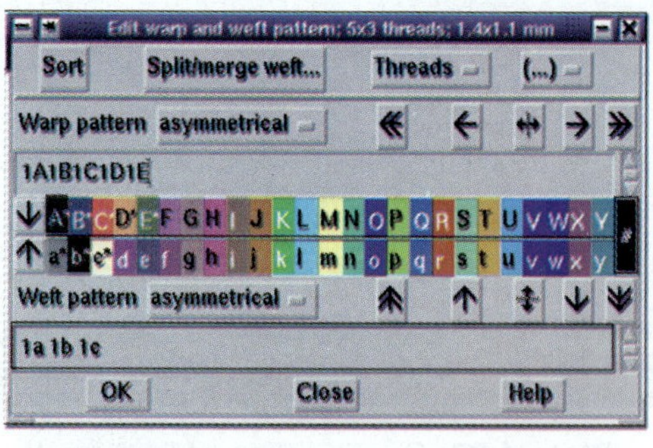

Plate 4.38: A software for creative use of colours in a design/pattern

Plate 4.39: Use of CAD/CAM technology for designing

PLATES SECTION—V

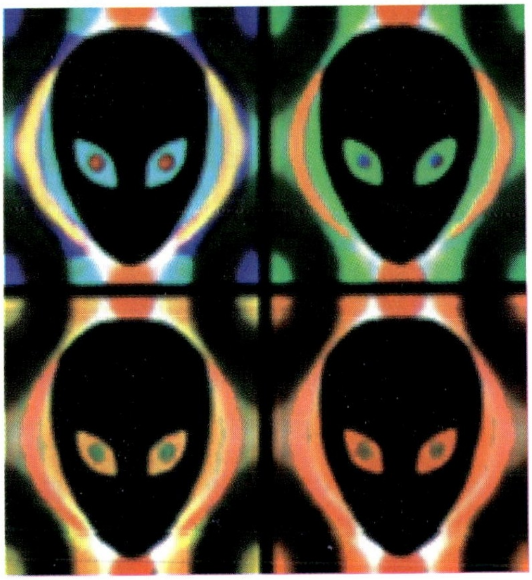

Plate 5.1: An illuminative/reftlective print on a techno textile

Plate 5.2: Banana fabric (green textile)

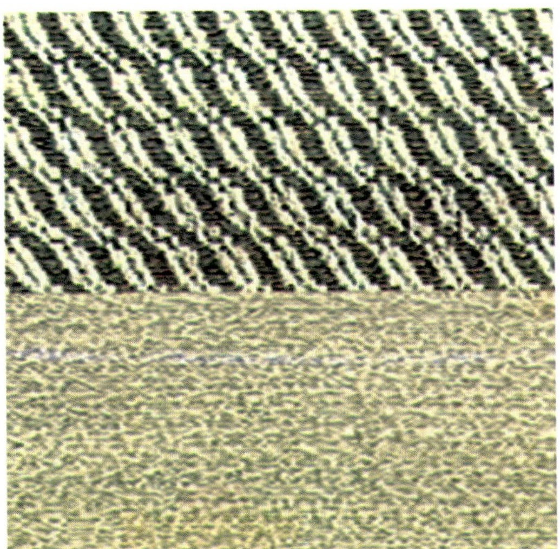

Plate 5.3: Organic hemp fabric

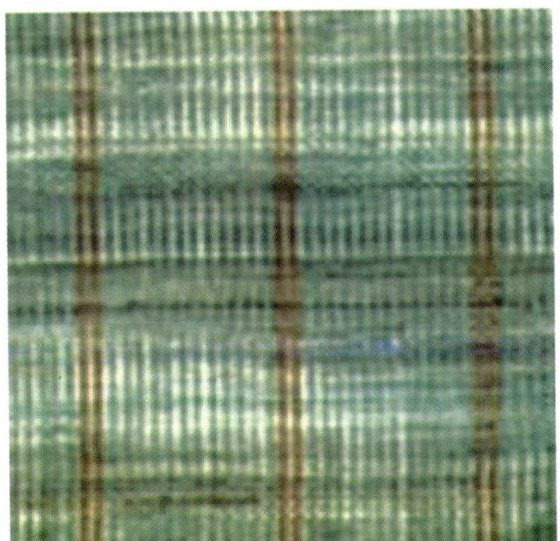

Plate 5.4: Leaf fibre fabric

Plate 5.5: Best ranked banana fabric of the study conducted (top, yoke, blouse)